LUIS BUÑUEL
A SYMPOSIUM

Papers given at
Trinity and All Saints' College
12-14 November 1982

Edited by Margaret A. Rees

LEEDS
Trinity and All Saints' College

Published 1983 by Trinity and All Saints' College
(Affiliated with the University of Leeds)
Brownberrie Lane
Horsforth
Leeds
LS18 5HD

British Library Cataloguing in Publication Data

Luis Buñuel.
1. Buñuel, Luis - Criticism and interpretation - Congresses
I. Rees, Margaret A.
863'.5 PQ6603.B/

ISBN 0 9507984 4 4

Produced at T.A.S.C., Leeds

CONTENTS

FOREWORD

The earlier series of annual conferences from which our Buñuel weekend sprang was organised by the Leeds University Spanish department in conjunction with the department at Trinity and All Saints' College, and the same collaboration gave rise to the papers reproduced here. The original idea for a three-day orgy of films by and talks on Buñuel came from Professor Gareth Davies, and he has generously arranged a contribution towards the cost of publication.

Not only did the papers themselves seem worth preserving, but in their published form they will serve to remind conference members of other factors such as the invaluable contribution made to the weekend as a whole by the lively enthusiasm of students from Newcastle, Swansea and York as well as from our local institutions; and also the slightly surreal moment when it became clear that there had been sent to us for our Buñuel weekend the very different version of Diary of a Chambermaid by a French director.

We should like to thank Dr H.M. Hallaway, Principal of the College, for encouraging us in the organisation of the conference.

Our thanks go also to Miss Nicola Mooney, who is as able a linguist as she is a typist, for her work on the typescript.

Margaret A. Rees

THAT OBSCURE OBJECT OF BELIEF

The discreet Catholicism of Luis Buñuel

I

Buñuel was educated by the Jesuits and so it is fitting that we should begin this weekend with something borrowed from Ignatius's Spiritual Exercises. Before passing on to our more intellectual and metaphysical considerations it is a good idea to create an atmosphere, a mood, a suitable climate, what is called a 'composition of place'. In order to bring about these conditions spiritual writers recommend the assistance of an image, a holy picture. We shall do just this and use as our image, our picture, Un Chien Andalou. In this film we have already present most of the obsessions, situations and comments that are found in his subsequent work. In a sense he has only made one film (or perhaps two: Un Chien Andalou and L'Age d'Or). His later works are remakes and revisions of this. It is of course the opening sequence that sticks in the memory and is liable to shock us even today. Its power is remarkable, since unlike the modern horror film an impact is made without any special effects but simply by the use of the camera and montage. It shows us the sort of powerful response the camera can elicit. Looking at pictures is not a purely passive thing. We create a world of our own through the mind's ability to associate and connect separate images. Ian Walker, in 'Buñuel's Half Century', an article in Sight and Sonnd (Winter 1977-78), analysed this opening scene and showed how twelve brief shots are so put together that the mind jumps to conclusions and makes its own connections often on the basis of insufficient evidence. So, if we are frightened we have frightened ourselves, if we are disgusted we have disgusted ourselves. In the same way we frighten ourselves in a nightmare. A more recent example of Buñuel making the mind jump to conclusions is to be found in The Phantom of Liberty. There is the scene with the postcards: the man in the park showing the postcards to the little girls, the reaction of the mother on finding them in the possession of her daughter, the feelings aroused by them in husband and wife ... all these lead us to draw a conclusion that is unwarranted and we experience a shock when we see that they are only views of buildings in Paris. It is this mysterious power of the mind that lies behind artistic creation. The artist is the one who 'only connects', who sees relationships that others do not see. Once he has presented them, others either make this new connection along with him or they are reminded of something they have already experienced deep down but have been unable to articulate. Man is a creator because he has this power of association. This was one of the messages of the surrealists. By placing together objects hitherto not associated - 'the chance meeting upon a dissecting table of a sewing machine and an umbrella' - something new and wonderful and beautiful was born. The surrealists called attention to this neglected truth at a time when art was suffering from convention and a surfeit of stale images. The surrealists were fond of juxtaposing objects on canvas in such a way that the viewer experienced feelings of absurdity, horror, wonder, pleasure, laughter or rage. This is the art of collage. The photograph can be used in an even more effective way since it has a greater air of similitude. There is such a thing as 'trick' photography. Perhaps we can recall those booths at the fair where you could put your head through a hole and be photographed with someone else's body. That there is such a thing as a funny photograph indicates the existence of a release of creative power. But with the moving camera (where of course nothing really moves, there is simply a series of stills into which the human mind projects movement because of the imperfection of the eye and its inability to make distinctions) ... with the moving camera one can break the bonds of time. Un Chien Andalou is an example of this. 'Once upon a time' it begins, and we are in fairy-story time which is no time at all but the eternal myth, the perennial, the ever true, the reality that the demands of the clock and the routine of everyday life seek to destroy. This film tries to liberate us by destroying the usual time sequence. The watch worn on the wrist is brusquely swept aside. We pass from 'eight years later' to 'around three o'clock in the morning' to 'sixteen years before' to 'in the springtime'. By breaking down the time barrier as well as the space barrier we are not destroying reality but only a pseudo-reality. We are being liberated so that we can step into the great mystery of being. The mystery that is sometimes glimpsed in dreams and visions. Truth is more important than plausibility. Truth is often stranger than fiction. The odd events in a Buñuel film are as nothing compared with the strange things that are recorded in the sucesos page of ABC. Here are a few: 'Corta una oreja de su amigo y se come como "tapa". La victima no reaccionó ante el ataque de su compañero de chateo'. 'Las cucarachas, método para anunciar terremotos'. 'Captura una trucha en su huerta de tomates'. 'Muerde a un policía y se queda sin dentadura'. '"Jesucristo", "Pilatos" y la "Magdalena" detenidos por alterar el orden público'. 'Los gatos se mueren de tristeza'. This is the sort of news we want to hear. The simplest form of transcending time is to be found in the flashback which Buñuel uses with great effect in El, but for its most sophisticated form we have to go to Last Year in Marienbad. As Godard so rightly said, every film has a beginning, a middle and an end - but not necessarily in that order. After the moving picture came the talking picture but unfortunately most films miss the opportunities afforded by sound for making a creative re-association. Sound is too often conventional and illustrative of what one sees on the screen. However in the sound track that Buñuel added later to Un Chien Andalou we have an example of a positive use of sound. The romantic love duet of Tristan and Isolde accompanies the androgyne toying with the disembodied hand. Later on, Buñuel gave us the Hallelujah Chorus as an accompaniment to the orgy in his film Viridiana. The artist then is like the anarchist who destroys man-made order so as to preserve reality. He is like the surrealist and the freudian who seek to liberate man and allow him to love and appreciate the mystery at the heart of reality.

There are other inhibitions and constraints besides space and time. Our lives are compartmentalised, we are separated from each other by sex. Sex is often non-communication, an obstacle to understanding since it divides humanity into two opposing camps, there is often a war between the sexes. But in reality there is no complete or total division between male and female, the normal person partakes of both sexes. There is a whole area of indeterminate, unresolved sexuality, a shadowy region into which we enter when we contemplate the androgynous figure down in the street in Un Chien Andalou. Transvestism and fetishism (feet, shoes, legs) are often found in other Buñuel films and fetishism reminds us that sex is operative even where there is no possibility of sexual reproduction. Perversion has a theoretic interest for him since it says something about sex that 'normality' cannot account for.

Un Chien Andalou introduces us into this real mysterious world and its hidden forces that convention, society and respectability are continually seeking to destroy because they cannot understand or control it. This is the mystery at the heart of reality, the real mystery and not that little box with stripes which we carry around and clutch so closely to us.

II

Before we pass on from this composition of place to our meditation proper, we should remind ourselves that there is nothing particularly Spanish about Un Chien Andalou, not even the title which is in French. The tango which forms a sort of theme-tune is Argentinian and that is not the same thing at all. Neither is there anything especially Catholic about the film - apart from the two unfortunate Marist brothers who are dragged along as part of the detritus of the past. Sometimes the Spanish and Catholic elements in Buñuel distract us from the real meaning of what we see, since it is easy to read into the film our preconceptions about Spain and the Roman Catholic Church. But Buñuel's films are about the human situation, something that is wider and more universal than either Spain or the Church on earth.

III

So let us begin our analysis.

(1) In nearly all the films the Church and Catholicism appear somewhere, this is inevitable considering the sort of person Buñuel is, his background and education and the situations and characters

he is portraying. The drums which were beaten incessantly during the last days of Holy Week in the village of Calanda where he spent his childhood, re-echo through his films. There is the drum roll at the end of *Nazarín*, their rhythm is taken up in *El* with the rattling of the stair rod, and their noise is replicated at the end of *That Obscure Object of Desire*. Since the Church was part of his Aragonese upbringing he can be said to be culturally a Catholic. In his autobiography, *Mon Dernier Soupir*, he not only speaks of his love for the *retablos* in Spanish cathedrals and the peace and calm of a Spanish cloister, he also slips into Catholic and Christian categories like 'the seven capital sins'. So his Catholicism is not just dragged into his films for the sake of effect, it is often introduced non-judgementally. Just as it is true that in order to understand Spanish literature and history and politics, one has to know something about Catholicism, so too, to understand Buñuel's films. The priests drinking their chocolate in *Tristana*, the flash-back to the communion scene in *Belle de Jour*, the church scenes in *El* - all these are part of a religious background and come to his mind effortlessly. Often these references have their humour, like Jesus wanting to shave off his beard in *Vía Láctea*, and there are some who would categorise these scenes as blasphemous. Maybe, but only blasphemous in the way in which this is common in a Catholic culture. Jokes about the Church and holy persons are frequent and do not create that *frisson* they sometimes do with English Catholics. Sometimes critics take far too seriously and sententiously this background Catholicism that is present in most of his films.

(2) However there are other images and incidents which are not the conventional reactions we would expect from the normal Catholic. At times Christian imagery is used in a disconcerting fashion. The use of Da Vinci's 'Last Supper' to illustrate an orgy, Millet's 'Angelus' to contrast the world of work and honest labour favourably with those who waste their time in prayer. At times we seem to be in looking-glass land. The character of El has something of the jealous God who wants to possess us totally, who can brook no rival, who lives in a fantastic art nouveau house, whose demands are unreasonable - not entirely dissimilar to the God who made total demands on Teresa of Avila. El admits to some faults but the one he will not tolerate being accused of, is injustice. In this film religion and paranoia are related since the paranoiac is the one who interprets all reality in the sense of his obsession. In The Exterminating Angel we have the reverse situation to that of the parable in the Gospel. It is not those who are invited to the banquet who are saved, but those servants who have the good sense to leave the house before the banquet takes place. Then there is Buñuel's treatment of the blind and maimed, so different from what is common among Christians today. For him, as indeed for the Bible, physical disease is often a sign of man's moral illness, his alienation from society and God. The physical degeneration of the beggars in Viridiana and Los Olvidados is not a thing to be pitied. And when the young thugs in the latter film beat up these miserable creatures they are in some perverse way making a stand for decency. Buñuel, like many deaf people, has an aversion to the blind, and those who cannot see are often for him a symbol of evil. He admits to this in Mon Dernier Soupir (p. 272) and recalls with pleasure a phrase of Benjamin Péret, 'Isn't mortadella made by

blind people?'. But to compensate this, Buñuel likes dwarfs. Not only are they reputed to have great sexual prowess but they are usually content with what they are and accept life with good grace and a shrug of the shoulders.

(3) But there are some films of Buñuel that are more explicit about Catholicism, in which it is the theme rather than the background or the subject of incidental comment. Rather special in this class is La Voie Lactée (Vía Láctea, The Milky Way). In this film he compresses into one artistic unity a history of Catholic theology in a similar way to that in which Un Chien Andalou gives us in fifteen minutes the history of an individual. It is a story in pictures of the Church and its conflict with heresy. It is about certainty: the certainty of Catholicism and the certainty of heretics. Both claim to possess the truth. It can be put alongside Menéndez y Pelayo's Historia de los Heterodoxos.

The form of the film is similar to the picaresque novel. It is a road-film about the journey of two modern pilgrims, tramps, to Compostella. It tells of the people they meet on the way - a mad curé, a Catholic school where teachers and pupils recite anathemas during a picnic, a restaurant where the waiters discuss the Incarnation in the interval of serving at table, a priest instructing a couple before marriage who has to bilocate since they are in separate bedrooms. Then there is a dream of the Pope being executed by a band of anarchists - the sound of the shot being audible at the picnic. There are several appearances of Our Lady and a meeting with one of the demons who describes hell in terms of Luis de Granada's Guide of Sinners. All this is cut into by incidents, real and imaginary, from the life of Christ. Buñuel draws on church history for a secret meeting of the followers of Priscillián in the forest, the Inquisition in session, a Jansenist and a Jesuit engaged in a fencing duel, a nun being nailed to a cross in her convent, the disinterment and burning of the remains of a bishop discovered after his death to have had heretical opinions. All the incidents from church history are based on fact but by free association and neglect of the time sequence they are seen to be not merely events-over-and-forgotten, but actually operative at the present time. Any loss of plausibility only makes the lesson stronger. Catholicism is thus seen to be a living thing but the apparent incongruities and contradictions are not necessarily, in Buñuel's world, an argument against Catholicism. Rather than an attack on the Church the film is a statement about the Church and how its history affects the present. But it is an interesting film because it is not merely a statement about the behaviour of Christians, it also concerns their beliefs. Here we are presented with the six central mysteries of the Catholic religion.

(a) At the beginning of the film the innkeeper explains the presence of Christ in the Eucharist as being like the presence of the hare in the pâté, at which point the priest accuses him of being a '<u>pâtelier</u>'. The viewer may be tempted to laugh at this but it is a serious comment since there were some sixteenth-century heretics who actually used the example of the hare in the pâté to explain eucharistic theology. The priest after quoting Tertullian, 'Credo quia absurdum', says that we have to take Christ's words literally since religion is about mystery, without mystery there would be no religion.

(b) The incident in the forest with the followers of Priscillián which is all spoken in Latin with French subtitles concerns the origins of evil and that dualism between spirit, the work of God who is good, and body, the work of the devil which is bad. Some actually did argue that the body should be punished and despised to the extent of submitting it to the pleasures of the flesh, hence the orgy that follows.

(c) At the restaurant, after the head waiter has dismissed the possibility of there being any real atheists, the conversation turns to the divinity of Christ. We are struck by the incongruity of modern servants engaging in this kind of small talk. But it is not so absurd as it might seem since the original disputes about Arianism were conducted not by academic theologians but by ordinary (though rather subtle) Greeks of the fourth century.

(d) The bishop whose body is exhumed because of the discovery of his heretical writings provides an occasion for a consideration of the doctrine of the Trinity and the recitation of parts of the Athanasian Creed where each statement appears to the unthinking person to be contradicted by the one that follows.

(e) The problem of man's free will is contested by the Jansenist and Jesuit and their dialectic skills are aptly portrayed by the duel they engage in.

(f) Throughout the film the figure of the Virgin Mary appears at times in unexpected and incongruous situations - as indeed it does in the Roman Catholic religion.

Now it is this treatment of the mysteries of Catholicism that is significant. Often theologians seem to reduce mystery to a series of formulas suitable for inclusion in a catechism. But during this film it seems as if Buñuel is implying that the trouble with Catholicism is that it is not mysterious enough. He himself does not fall into such an error as the end of the film leaves us hanging in the air. There is doubt whether the bones at Compostella are really those of St James, perhaps they are somebody else's, Priscillián for instance? The last act of Jesus in the film is to cure two blind men. But does he cure them? and what is blindness? Jesus steps over a narrow trench in the ground quite naturally, so do his disciples, they almost skip over it. Then comes the turn of the two who have had their sight restored. They are unable to cross it, they tap the ground with their sticks as they did before. Do they lack faith? Many interpretations are open. No Buñuel film really ends, there is always an unanswered question, he never leaves the customer satisfied. Is that what the Church should be like? It is clear from other films and from what he says in his autobiography that Vatican II leaves him nonplussed. The figure of the Bishop/Gardener in The Discreet Charm of the Bourgeoisie, the discussion between the Carmelite friars in The Phantom of Liberty about the demotion of certain saints and the rehabilitation of Savonarola, and his remarks in Mon Dernier Soupir about how changed he found his old Jesuit college when he revisited it - all indicate that he is rather lost in a desacralised Church. Were he to attend a modern Catholic church service he would doubtless miss the kissing of the priest's hand by the altar boys, the veiling of women's heads and even faces, the countless statues many of them dressed in real dresses - there is nothing very erotic about our new liturgy.

(4) Buñuel's Vía Láctea is exceptional. In most films where he takes religion as the main theme, it is not to give an overview of the history of Christianity but to present a particular story which provides an occasion for his saying what he feels about the important things of life, and this often involves a criticism of Catholicism and the religion he was brought up in as a child. Nazarín, Viridiana, Simón en el Desierto are stories about three people whose lives are bound up in the institutional Church. Each has a vocation and each film tells of the corrosive effect of this vocation on the life of the individual. There is no lack of sympathy for these individuals (he says that Nazarín is one of his favourite films) and so the attack on the Church is more subtle than it is for instance in The Exterminating Angel and in the portrayal of such characters as Archibaldo de la Cruz and El who are examples of how religion can lead to paranoia. What is under scrutiny in these three is more than the institutional Church or its official doctrines. He is attacking the idea of Christianity itself. The absurdities, unhappiness and suffering are not due to the malfunctioning of a system and its failure to attain its ideal - it is the ideal itself that is at fault. So we are no longer dealing with a cultural or behavioural criticism, but with a radical attack in the manner of Sade. In Nazarín (1958) a priest sets out to lead a life of dedication to the service of the poor but not only fails to bring about any betterment in the ways of the wicked but seems by his very goodness or naïvety to be a source of dissension and strife among the people with whom he finds himself. He also fails in that he manages to inspire love towards himself and not towards God in those whom he befriends. In a scene Buñuel interpolates into the Galdós story from Sade, Nazarín fails to persuade a dying woman to turn to God and away from her lover. In the end he doubts

his own ability to distinguish between good and evil. A good life or a bad life come to the same thing. The film ends on an ambiguous note. There are reminiscences of Christ's journey to Calvary in Nazarín's arrest and way to execution. But he does not end up by being crucified but by accepting the offer of a pineapple from an ordinary woman. Is he at last ceasing to be self-centred and recognising his own needs and that they can only be met by another human being? Christianity begins with an apple in a garden and ends on a cross and resurrection; Nazarín begins with a crucified life and ends by accepting a pineapple.

In Viridiana (1961) we find a female version of the same theme. She fails to prevent and is in some way responsible for the suicide of her uncle Don Jaime because she cannot respond to his love. Sexual love - even incestuous sexual love - might have saved her as it might have saved Nazarín if he had responded to Andara and Beatriz. Her works of charity towards the beggars and outcasts only result in the destruction of the family home and of themselves in the orgy at the end of the film. The Christian way of life like the crucifix has a blade concealed within it, a blade that can kill. Doing good in Viridiana's way is like setting free the dog from under the cart - pointless because there is always another captive to replace the one you have freed. It is best to give up the Christian life and throw the crown of thorns on the fire and learn how to play cards in a ménage à trois.

Simón (1965) although incomplete and more genial in its treatment, is in the end just as nihilistic. There are several amusing touches; the rich man Praxedes getting a new column built for Simón; the thief whose hands are miraculously restored using them immediately to box a child's ears; the she-devil disguised first as a schoolgirl and then as the good shepherd (with the hefty kick she gives to the little lamb).

But in the end Simón is removed from his pillar to a modern skyscraper and finds himself in a discothèque. There is here the same message as in Nazarín and Viridiana. Life is too precious to be spent in religious pursuits. In Mon Dernier Soupir, Buñuel finds a perfect expression of his philosophy of life in the Book of Wisdom, chapter 2, vv. 2-7 (of course for Buñuel, brought up a Catholic, Wisdom is a canonical book of the Bible!),

> Short and sorrowful is our life, and there is no remedy when a man comes to his end, and no one has been known to return from Hades. Because we were born by mere chance, and hereafter we shall be as though we had never been; because the breath in our nostrils is smoke, and reason is a spark kindled by the beating of our hearts. When it is extinguished, the body will turn to ashes, and the spirit will dissolve like empty air. Our name will be forgotten in time, and no one will remember our works; our life will pass away like the traces of a cloud, and be scattered like mist that is chased by the rays of the sun and overcome by its heat. For our allotted time is the passing of a shadow, and there is no return from our death, because it is sealed up and no one turns back. Come therefore let us enjoy the good things that exist, and make use of the creation to the full as in youth. Let us take our fill of costly wines and perfumes, and let no flower of spring pass by us. Let us crown ourselves with rosebuds before they wither. Let none of us fail to share in our revelry, everywhere let us leave signs of enjoyment, because this is our portion, and this our lot.

These words put in the mouth of the wicked are according to Buñuel at the root of his atheism. However, one has to note that these remarks are but a further step on the road from attitudes that are fairly common among Catholics. The road begins with the mild scepticism that takes religion with a pinch of salt, knowing full well that Christian revelation does not give us in this life the last word that can be said, and often the Church and its members get things a little wrong. This is a Catholic scepticism born of a sense of proportion and a realisation of the essential obscurity of faith. It is linked to a Catholic sense of irony and often associated with the typically Spanish desengaño which in its turn is related to the sense of man's nothingness, as one finds in John of the Cross. It is part of the tradition of negative theology that realises that we can more easily say what God is not, than what he is. That is how the road begins, but with Buñuel it ends in a sort of nihilism.

(5) What exactly is the nature of Buñuel's atheism? He himself identifies it with that of Sade. But for all his avowal that God is no longer a problem for him because God does not exist, he is much more preoccupied with the 'God problem' than any British or American film-maker. That it should be necessary to devote a chapter of his autobiography to his atheism is remarkable, it might even suggest that there is a bit of paranoia here. Padre Alcalá in his book Buñuel, cine e ideología discusses Buñuel's loss of faith, suggesting that it is a rejection of the image of God he gained in childhood from his family and school, especially the Jesuit schooling at El Salvador in Zaragoza. Such a giving up of religion is found in many Spaniards who reject the idea of a stern God sitting in judgment on man, an idea which often turns his believers into monsters or madmen. There is also a dislike of the alliance of the Church with other forms of authority that restrict a man's freedom. There is nothing very new about these observations, but Alcalá relates them to Astete's catechism which reduced the teaching of the Church to a collection of formulas and he notes that by Buñuel's day, this catechism had run to 550 editions, equalling that of the Bible. He calls Astete 'la columna vertebral de la formación religiosa y

católica de Buñuel'.

But this does not go far enough since Buñuel's position is more than just having an imperfect image of God. Many others have this and have been able to correct it in later life. Not so Buñuel. He is a surrealist and so he believes that chance is the great reality at the heart of things. His later films, The Discreet Charm, The Phantom of Liberty and That Obscure Object are surrealist in so far as they follow the logic of dreams or the stream of consciousness and there is only a haphazard connection between the events they record. Because he believes in chance he has no time for Providence. This is the message behind The Exterminating Angel whose original title was 'Los náufragos de la Calle de Providencia'. Once man allows himself to think that he is under the control of a higher power then he loses his freedom to act and he has to have recourse to all manner of magical devices to extricate himself from a situation he himself has brought about by his belief. Buñuel maintains that we are ourselves when we assert our freedom. This is close to Sartre's position. In his memoirs Buñuel recalls several incidents from his life in Mexico showing how in this country one comes across pure surreal acts, pure assertions of human freedom with no other apparent motive. A man goes to No 39 of a certain street and asks for Señor Sánchez. The concierge replies that he doesn't know any Señor Sánchez, try at No 41. He goes to 41 and makes the same request. The concierge there says there is no one of that name here, try 39, the first concierge must have made a mistake as that's where Sr Sánchez lives. He returns to 39 and explains what has happened. The concierge asks him to wait a moment. He goes to his room, gets a revolver, returns and shoots the enquirer dead. When asked later about his motive he says: I killed him because he was asking me too many questions. A true story illustrative of the autonomy of human action. It is better to act than not act at all. This attitude is related to the nihilism we have considered in _Nazarín_, _Viridiana_ and _Simón_ where Buñuel asserts that good and bad are all the same. Such a belief in chance and in complete lack of purpose is a rejection of Providence and God himself. Buñuel does not reject God as many do, because there is evil in the world and the existence of evil is considered to be incompatible with God. For him evil and good come to the same thing. There is no purpose, all is chance, so there can be no God. But his atheism rooted in surrealism is a qualified atheism. He repeats 'Thank God I am an atheist'. But this qualification 'Thank God' is by way of a further denial or rejection of God. He argues that if God were to exist he could not possibly be concerned about us and so as far as we are concerned he might just as well not exist. So his 'Thank God I am an atheist' is not contradictory, it is barring the door against God, it is a double atheism, his existence is irrelevant to us. This would seem to be the exact position that the _Book of Wisdom_ is describing as the ultimate rejection. Moreover the idea of God not being in the least interested in the human race is in utter contradiction to the Christian Gospel. So here we have the complete mirror image of Christianity.

But unfortunately (or fortunately) the matter does not end here. Buñuel complicates the situation by linking chance with its brother (twin) Mystery. His atheism because it is rooted in chance, because it is surreal, leads him to the acceptance of the inexplicable. All our universe is mystery, he says in _Mon Dernier Soupir_ (pp. 214-5). He has a horror of understanding everything. This brings us back to _Vía Láctea_, where his portrayal of Christian mysteries is negative because they seem to make things too plain. So for him chance, since it is closely related to mystery, is a positive thing. It leads to awe, to wonder. Alcalá (p. 140) refers to a statement of Buñuel dating from 1965; 'En la época de mi juventud miraba al cielo y me decía a mí mismo: Es bonito, pero allá arriba no hay nada. Hoy me digo simplemente: ¡Qué bonito!' Now such a position when confronted with reality is not necessarily incompatible with Christianity. It is not necessarily a denial of Providence. It could simply be a denial of some of the weird things human beings make Providence do. In an interview in May 1960 Buñuel stated: 'Creo que hay que buscar a Dios en el hombre'. J. F. Aranda takes this and similar remarks and declares: 'Buñuel ha sido uno de los pensadores españoles más alejado de lo eterno, pero su obra busca los valores permanentes del hombre'. But since Vatican II and Gaudium and Spes this is not at all obvious as we are told (Part I, Chapter 1, § 12): 'According to the almost unanimous opinion of believers and unbelievers alike, all things on earth should be related to man as their centre and crown'. It all depends whether this flight to man and human values is a flight from mystery or a flight to mystery. It was St Augustine who said that man is a mystery <u>in</u> himself and <u>to</u> himself and it is in that inward journey that we touch on the mystery that sustains us all. Our opening remarks about the artistic experience and <u>Un Chien Andalou</u> are relevant here.

No human being is completely consistent and Buñuel for all his nihilism is the most mild of men. His quotation from the <u>Book of Wisdom</u> stops short at Verse 9. He does not tell us that Verse 10 says: 'Let us oppress the righteous poor man; let us not spare the widow nor regard the grey hairs of the aged. But let our might be our law of right, for what is weak proves itself to be useless'. He likes firearms but does not kill people and if there is a spider in the house he will call for his wife to kill it. In Mon Dernier Soupir we are told of his feelings towards death and we can see the deep humanity and humility of this man before the greatest mystery of all. Gone for him are the supports of the death of Christ, the crucifix, the Dolorosa and her tears, they no longer mean anything. But the enjoyment and worship of life and that elusive reality that is shown in films like Discreet Charm, Phantom of Liberty and Obscure Object continues. He does believe in honesty and personal morality as well as chance which is the twin of mystery. So that one can understand the remark of his Dominican priest friend who after a spell of argument with him on religion and atheism said to him: 'Before I met you I sometimes felt my faith to be growing weak, but after we have been talking together, my faith is reaffirmed'. Faith and no-faith the same thing?

As his last trick Buñuel considers it would be fun to summon all his atheist friends to his death-bed, but also a priest, and then to make his confession. This would be the biggest scandal of all time. His one regret in dying is not to know what's going on in the world he has left, and as a last wish he would like to be allowed occasionally to go to the nearest kiosk and buy a newspaper and then with paper under his arm to return to the cemetery and read it in the quiet of the tomb.

M. E. WILLIAMS

Trinity and All Saints' College
Leeds

ON BUÑUEL'S DIARY OF A CHAMBERMAID

Between July and August, 1963, Buñuel worked with Jean-Claude Carrière in Madrid on the shooting script for Diary of a Chambermaid and made the film in and around Paris during the winter of 1963-64. It belongs, then, to an intense and fertile period of activity in Buñuel's cinematic production. Viridiana was completed in 1961, The Exterminating Angel in 1962, Simon of the Desert in 1965, and Belle de Jour in 1966. Diary of a Chambermaid, not surprisingly, has much in common with, in particular, Viridiana, The Exterminating Angel and Belle de Jour. It is also important to remember that, after the completion of The Exterminating Angel in 1962, Buñuel's intention had been to shoot not Diary in Paris but Tristana in Madrid. He had completed the script with Julio Alejandro, hired his actors and chosen his locations. At the last moment, taking revenge for the scandal caused by Viridiana two years earlier, the Spanish censorship intervened and stopped the film, using the convenient argument that the script included approving references to duelling, which contravened the new code of censorship. Failing to make Tristana, which he eventually made in 1970, Buñuel toyed with one or two projects before falling back on an old idea: Diary of a Chambermaid. In a sense, then, the film became a substitute for Tristana. In the following discussion illuminating parallels can be made between the two films, while important points of contact can also be established with the other films already mentioned. [1]

Another factor which links three of the films in question is their derivation from novels. *Belle de Jour*, for instance, is an adaptation of Joseph Kessel's novel of the same name which Buñuel claimed did not please him in the least. *Tristana* is based on the novel of that name by the nineteenth-century Spanish novelist, Benito Pérez Galdós. And *Diary of a Chambermaid* takes as its source the similarly titled novel by Octave Mirbeau published in 1900. In adapting the novels, Buñuel, as might be expected, made significant changes in order to underline his own themes and ideas. *Tristana* is an interesting case in point, particularly in relation to its ending. In novel and film the bourgeois uncle - in Galdós Don Juan, in Buñuel Don Lope - takes the young, beautiful, orphaned Tristana into his care and she later becomes his mistress. In novel and film Tristana has an affair with a painter and in both she develops a tumour of the leg which requires its amputation. Galdós presents her finally married to Don Juan, settling for her lot, albeit with a certain resignation, and making puddings for a delighted husband. Buñuel's ending is much more bitter in all respects. Tristana's amputated leg makes her much more clearly her husband's prisoner, as his own words testify: 'A woman of honour, a crippled leg, and in the house' (*La mujer honrada, pierna quebrada y en casa*) (46).[2] She, asserting herself much more strongly than Galdós's heroine, denies her husband his sexual rights and finally escapes his clutches when, after he suffers a heart attack, she allows him to die, exposing him to the icy wind from the open window. But that window, opening onto a winter landscape, is simultaneously a mirror on Tristana's future, for there cannot be much in prospect for a woman as physically mutilated and as spiritually harsh as she has now become. Buñuel's ending, reinforcing changes elsewhere in the film, serves to underline very powerfully his portrayal of the stultifying, soul-destroying effects of a narrow-minded bourgeois society in which men and women alike are cripples.

What, then, were Buñuel's changes in relation to Mirbeau's novel? The novel is a first-person narrative in which Célestine gives an account of her life as a maid in the service of the Lanlaires, a bourgeois couple who live in a large house. During her time with them she flirts with a Captain who lives next door, an eccentric figure who has a passion for eating flowers and who at one point is maliciously encouraged by Célestine to devour his pet ferret. Subsequently, Célestine has an affair with the coachman, Joseph, whom she knows to have raped and killed a young girl, they marry and, after he has stolen the Lanlaires' silver, they escape to Cherbourg where they open a café. Such are the main events of the novel. Around them, though, Mirbeau wove an intricate and largely shapeless pattern of incidents which consist of Célestine's recollections of her previous employers. They include her employment by an old lady to keep her tubercular grandson happy and a period in the service of an elderly foot fetishist. In the central narrative and the subordinate incidents Mirbeau's main objective was, as one critic has observed, 'to show the depravity of <u>les maîtres</u>, the abominable conditions of life below stairs, and the inevitable corruption of the servants by their masters'.[3] In consequence, Célestine's role is an essentially passive one, for Mirbeau uses her as a largely dispassionate observer of the numerous events in which she becomes involved.

Buñuel's hatred of the bourgeoisie - of the establishment and its representatives - evidently drew him to Mirbeau's novel, but the film is, in a narrative sense, much more shapely and concise, focusing wholly on the Monteil family (Mirbeau's Lanlaires), their servants and the Captain. Mirbeau's foot fetishist - merely a former employer - is now Madame Monteil's father, an indication of the film's pulling together of the novel's looser threads. Other characters and incidents are also subjected to important changes. The Captain who lives next door is, though still eccentric, no longer a flower-eater. Célestine has an affair with Joseph but does not marry him. Instead, learning of his violation and murder of the young girl, she denounces him to the police and takes the Captain as her husband. In short, Buñuel's Célestine ceases to be merely an observer of events around her and assumes a much more active role. Another significant difference between the novel and the film has to do with Buñuel's fascination with the subconscious, the inner lives of his characters, and in this respect Rabour, Madame Monteil, Joseph and Célestine herself are particularly striking creations, vastly superior to anything in the novel. Finally, Buñuel moved the action of the film from the end of the nineteenth century, where the events of the novel are located, to the mid-1920s, to a time, then, when the forces of fascism were on the march. In 1930 the showing of L'Age d'Or at the Studio 28 in Paris provoked violent attacks from the Young Catholics, the League of Patriots and the Anti-Jewish League. In response to pressure from the Right, Chiappe, the Chief of Police, banned Buñuel's film. In the final sequence of Diary of a Chambermaid the cries and slogans of a fascist demonstration are intermingled, significantly, with shouts of 'Long live Chiappe'. In other words, Buñuel's ending links the bourgeois characters and attitudes of the film's central narrative to those forces that would soon tear Europe apart. From the demonstration the camera moves to a stormy sky and a flash of lightning on which the word 'Fin' ominously appears.

In relation to sources, it is worth making (though not labouring) the point, that in 1946 Jean Renoir made Diary of a Chambermaid, also based on Mirbeau's novel, with Paulette Goddard as the lead. Renoir too pinpoints the vices of the bourgeoisie but his characters, unlike Buñuel's, are 'never conceived in acid'.[4] In the first half of the film, Renoir's Célestine is not unlike Buñuel's, refusing to be dominated by her masters. Subsequently, though, Renoir focuses not on the affair between Célestine and the servant, Joseph, but on her relationship with Georges, the Lanlaires' tubercular son. In the end he revolts against his bourgeois background and the final scene reveals him distributing the family silver to the crowd - a sentimental Hollywood ending that Buñuel could never conceive of. Indeed, the difference between Buñuel and Renoir as film-makers could not be greater. Freddy Buache observes that 'there is definitely a certain charm about Renoir's smooth, satin style', while Tom Milne states that 'as always with Renoir, it is the texture that counts'.[5] Buñuel's uncompromising aggression, his total lack of sentimentality, his fast, unfussy style, evident in all his films, exclude the possibility of any debt to Renoir.

As for the critics, Buñuel's film has attracted a variety of comment. The announcement that he would return to Paris to make the film with Jeanne Moreau created in Paris an atmosphere of great expectancy and the papers hinted at a treatment of the subject that would be truly sensational. In the event many critics were lukewarm, if that, in their reactions to the film. Jean-Louis Bory, writing in Arts, March 11, 1964, observed:

> This film, in the last resort ineffective in consequence of its timidity, and timid in consequence of its excessive realism, might have been saved if we could only recognize in it the imprint of Buñuel. This is notable by its absence, or its relative absence. Poetry is limited to the occasional revelation of a furtive bestiary: insects or wild animals. But where is the savagery in this film? Where is the eroticism?

In contrast, Claude Tarare, writing on the same day in L'Express, was effusive in his praise:

> This film, which is the culmination of Buñuel's work and which, in my view, is his masterpiece, has disappointed some of his most ardent fans. This is due, no doubt, to those aspects of the film I have already mentioned: its restraint, its almost classical moderation in its treatment of the subject matter, much more gentle and refined than in other films by the same director. The excellent dialogue of Jean-Claude Carrière ... contributes in no small measure to the strange effect of refinement which this fierce film produces.

Such were the contrasting viewpoints nearly twenty years ago. The passage of time, allowing for analysis and reflection, has on the whole allowed critics to appreciate the considerable qualities of Diary of a Chambermaid. Before proceeding to discuss it in detail, it is worth noting the assessment by Freddy Buache:

> It is a film, like several others directed by Buñuel, that is pejoratively classified as 'minor', which would imply that it is worthy of being judged alongside the countless other 'minor' run-of-the-mill films by other directors which sink rapidly into oblivion. This is really most unfair. Diary of a Chambermaid is an unequivocal statement, a warning, a political thesis, and a settling of accounts where Buñuel, with his customary humanism, creates the familiar dialectic of freedom, revolt and love. It stands like a light-house amidst the ink-black night of the French cinema. [6]

The principal preoccupations of Buñuel's cinema may be summarised briefly enough: freedom, instinct and passion on the one hand; repression, frustration and inhibition on the other. They are the themes which, in one form or another, link _L'Age d'Or_, made in 1930, and Buñuel's swan song, _That Obscure Object of Desire_, made in 1977. The themes take on, of course, particular concrete forms, fleshed-out images that we have come to recognize as characteristically Buñuelian. Repression and inhibition are thus identified with the forces of tradition both social and religious, with the bourgeoisie and with the Church. Freedom, often associated with instinctive or rebellious attitudes, tends to be embodied in particular individuals; the ecstatic lovers of _L'Age d'Or_, Séverine in _Belle de Jour_, Tristana in the film of that name. _Diary of a Chambermaid_ is, in relation to the above, a highly representative film and to that extent a profitable source of study. The theme of liberty, or the quest for personal freedom, is embodied in the chambermaid herself, and the film is very largely to do with the degree of her success or failure in obtaining it. Against her are arrayed the forces which seek to deny her freedom: above all, the bourgeois family by which she is employed; the social, sexual and political attitudes which they represent; and the extent to which they, tentacle-like, extend insidiously outwards to embrace destructively even the servants themselves. But _Diary_ merits our attention for other reasons too. It reveals as successfully as any other Buñuel film his understanding of and ability to communicate the complexity of human beings, in particular their secret, inner lives. It displays his great sense of wit and, with due respect to Jean-Claude Carrière, his splendid dialogue. And it is a fine example too - as illustrative in this respect as any other film - of Buñuel's wonderfully quick, simple yet illuminating cinema technique.

The opening sequence introduces us, through Célestine's eyes, to French provincial life and encapsulates in a few telling shots Buñuel's view of the bourgeoisie. Célestine notes the sad, neglected aspect of the countryside and then, as she reaches the town where she is to work, the deserted streets and the drawn blinds. The two details are significant. The neglected countryside, reminiscent of Don Jaime's decaying estate in Viridiana, points to the bourgeoisie's self-centredness, their introversion, their lack of responsibility to the land and those who work it for them. The drawn blinds suggest too the closed world of the bourgeoisie and anticipate those secretive activities practised by many of the film's characters behind locked doors. From the outset, hinting at self-indulgence and guilt-ridden secrecy, Buñuel sets out with clarity and precision some of the film's main themes.

Célestine's introduction to the small provincial town gives way to her introduction to the country house where she will work, and to her new employers, Monsieur Rabour and Monsieur and Madame Monteil. The large, expensively furnished house, be it in the country or the town, is a favourite Buñuel motif and is therefore to be found in many of his films: L'Age d'Or, Viridiana, The Exterminating Angel, Tristana, and a slight variation of it in Séverine's elegant apartment in Belle de Jour. In all these films the furniture and ornaments, as well as their owners' attitudes towards them, are revealed and displayed to us in detail and often, it should be emphasized, in close-up, so that they acquire the importance and prominence which they have for their bourgeois masters. Thus, through Célestine's guided tour of the house, Buñuel presents us with a mocking catalogue or inventory of bourgeois elegance, dwelling on individual objects in a manner which accords them the significance of sacred relics within the performance of bourgeois rites and rituals. The scenario reads:

> Now in the large drawing-room Madame Monteil walks towards a chest of drawers on which a number of different knick-knacks can be seen. A close-up to show them to us in detail: two porcelain figures and a snuffbox of shell and silver. [7]

The sitting-room is, indeed, a shrine or temple, entry into which can be achieved only when due reverence has been shown through the discarding of shoes:

> The two women reach the end of the small drawing-room where a doorway communicates with the large drawing-room. Without a word of explanation, Madame Monteil takes off her shoes. Célestine looks at her in amazement. [8]

The incident, presented by Buñuel with his usual dead-pan irony, illustrates the ritualistic formulae with which the bourgeoisie invest the ordinary activities of their lives. Incongruity, evident in Célestine's surprise, is a common Buñuel weapon which he employs not so much to bludgeon the bourgeoisie as to point to the empty repetitiveness of their lives and the dead, lifeless objects they worship.

The idea of ritual is strongly projected in Rabour, the elderly owner of the house. For him, as for Don Lope in Tristana, dress is part of a ritual that is reflected otherwise in almost every aspect of his life. Thus, for Rabour, dressing-gown and silk cravat are the insignia of bourgeois evenings spent at home, and when outside hat, gaiters and walking-stick become the emblems of solid respectability, of an image as refined and polished as the objects with which he adorns his house. Ritual, indeed, enslaves the bourgeoisie even in the darker, more secretive areas of activity, including private fetishes, and in this respect Rabour is a prime example. Consider his album of dirty postcards, neatly kept, scrutinized every evening behind locked doors, and also his collection of women's boots, carefully stored in a cupboard. And connected with the boots is the most important ritual of all, practised with all his previous female servants and now with Célestine. When she brings him his nightcap, he asks a favour of her: that she allow him to call her Marie; that she wear a pair of leather boots; and that she permit him to stroke her calf while she reads to him. Inasmuch as Rabour's practice is so clearly ritualistic, two important points can be made about it which are central to Buñuel's general presentation of bourgeois rites.

Firstly, the episode described above has evident religious overtones, which heighten its ritualistic character. Rabour's insistence on calling Célestine Marie brings to mind the Virgin Mary. Later, moreover, he kneels before her in a clear attitude of worship. It is worth recalling the episode in Tristana where Saturno, the deaf-mute, looks up at Tristana on the balcony, worshipping her beauty, and where, in the very next shot, the image of Tristana gives way to an image of the Virgin Mary. Buñuel's presentation of the incident involving Rabour and Célestine is clearly open to charges of blasphemy, but for Buñuel the blasphemy is all to do with love and nothing to do with religion. A further point of explanation is necessary. Rabour, it should be emphasized, is fascinated not by Célestine, a creature of flesh and blood, but by the boots, by objects which, like his dirty postcards, are dead and lifeless. The ritual objects of the bourgeoisie - be they items of furniture, ornaments or anything else - are, indeed, dead objects, and for Buñuel blasphemy lies in Rabour's worship of them in preference to the beautiful woman who stands before him. Such worship is, of course, destructive, for it is sterile and unrewarding. It is no accident, therefore, that Rabour is finally found dead in bed, embracing not the woman but the boots, a victim not of heroic passion but of an empty and destructive cause:

> ... on it [the bed] Monsieur Rabour is stretched out with the sheets rumpled and partly covering his nakedness. In his hand he is still clutching one of the boots. Monsieur Rabour is dead. [9]

Rabour's daughter, Madame Monteil, is as interesting a character as her father and in many respects, particularly in relation to her private obsessions, a true 'chip off the old block'. Her remark to Célestine that her father is 'cleanliness personified' (*la limpieza personificada*) (p. 22) throws a certain light on her own character, for events soon indicate that her life is a ritual of physical cleanliness. Our introduction to her reveals her to be a woman of about forty years of age, rather cold and, as the scenario indicates, with 'white skin' (*la piel blanca*) (p. 21). It is she, of course, who takes Célestine on the tour of the house, discarding her shoes prior to entry to the sitting-room and observing:

> Coming in from the garden, one always brings in some dirt on one's shoes ... [10]

In addition, she questions Célestine about her own cleanliness - 'One is to assume that you are very clean' (Así que es usted extremadamente limpia) (p. 22) - and insists that only she, Madame Monteil, is allowed to clean certain precious household objects. It is, though, her bathroom which is the true revelation. What activities go on there are anyone's guess - Buñuel at his typically malicious and subversive best leaves it to our imagination - but his camera intriguingly reveals dressing-table, washbasin, bidet, test tubes, flasks, retorts and bubbbling liquids. In short, as the scenario puts it, 'it seems more like a small chemical laboratory' (parece más bien un pequeño laboratorio químico) (p. 69). Cleanliness for Madame Monteil is clearly next to godliness, a ritual of physical purification.

What, then, of the lady's spiritual cleanliness? For her husband, Monteil, she has neither love, charity nor compassion. In one of Buñuel's most delightfully ironic scenes, a splendid exposure of bourgeois prudery, Madame Monteil confides to the priest that she is obliged to succumb to her husband's sexual demands at least twice a week, a revelation which offends both her and the priest's notion of seemliness (p. 81). When, later in the film, Monteil enters her bedroom, his intentions obvious, she coldly rejects him, prefering to continue with the empty ritual of combing her hair, and then dismisses him from the room. In another sequence, when Joseph and Célestine enter the sitting-room, Madame Monteil is preoccupied with the obsessive, ritualistic cleaning of her precious objects:

> In the large sitting-room Madame Monteil is engaged in the almost ritual cleaning of the fragile and precious objects which the room contains. She is near the display cabinet,

with a duster in her hand. She has taken off her shoes, in order not to dirty the carpet. 11

In a film of unpleasant characters Buñuel presents her as one of the most unpleasant - as clean as the lifeless objects with which she surrounds herself, and just as empty and as cold.

If his wife's fetish is physical cleanliness, Monteil's obsession is hunting. It is an occupation partly imposed upon him because, being powerless in the house where his wife and father-in-law reign supreme, he has nothing else to do. But Buñuel also associates hunting with self-centred and mindless bourgeois activities, just as earlier he has drawn attention to the impoverishment of the countryside as a consequence of bourgeois neglect. Buñuel's portrayal of Monteil is totally unflattering. The scenario reads:

Monsieur Monteil is a man of about forty years of age. He is tall and strong, a little florid. His face reveals a lack of will and, above all, of intelligence. He has neither importance nor authority in the house, where everything belongs to his father-in-law. He is a complete idler. 12

Considerable attention is given to Monteil's hunting bag and its contents. When we first see him, for example, he is returning from hunting, his gun on his shoulder, and he attempts to show the contents of the bag to his father-in-law (pp. 19-20). Later, as he leaves the house for a day's hunting, he takes the bag (p. 64). The point is this. A comparison can be drawn between Monteil and Rabour, between the contents of the younger man's bag - the dead animals that are his prime concern - and the boots that are the older man's obsession, for both are the lifeless objects of a ritual steadfastly pursued. Both men, moreover, have their uniforms - Rabour his dressing-gown and cravat, Monteil his gun and his hunter's outfit. If the boots are a comment on Rabour's sterile sexuality, the dead animals epitomize Monteil's purposeless sporting life. At one point Rabour blasts a butterfly with a shotgun. Monteil parallels him in relation to his shooting of the rabbits on the estate. For all their differences, both men indulge themselves in activities that are as inward-looking as they are destructive.

Monteil's other sport is his pursuit of women, an activity in which Buñuel shows him to be desperate, clumsy and pathetic. In relation to the activity as sport, it is not insignificant that Monteil should attempt to grab Célestine when he is dressed as a hunter, launching himself upon her as he would on some unsuspecting animal. Earlier he has stalked her avidly - '<u>Monteil follows her movements with a certain eagerness</u>' (<u>Monteil la sigue en sus movimientos con cierta avidez</u>) (p. 45) - and is encouraged by her provocative sensuality, but fails utterly to realize that it is she who is baiting him. Failing to snare Célestine, Monteil finally makes do with easier game - the docile Marianne, a girl who is totally inexperienced in the ways of the world. Before her the brave Monteil parades himself like a peacock - '<u>strutting about so that she can observe him better</u>' (<u>pavoneándose, para que ella pueda contemplarle mejor</u>) (p. 128). It is significant, moreover, that he should seduce Marianne behind the closed doors of the laundry. The camera lingers on the doors to remind us of the old Rabour flicking through his album behind the locked door of his room. Between the lifeless women of Rabour's postcards and the docile, submissive Marianne there is really little difference.

The Monteils' next-door neighbour is Captain Mauger, the eccentric paper-eater of Mirbeau's novel. Our introduction to him shows him throwing stones and rubbish into Monteil's garden and referring to the latter as 'That damned Monteil!' (¡Ese condenado de Monteil!) (p. 43). Initially, then, Mauger is portrayed as a rebel and, in particular, as a rebel against the bourgeoisie, for what has annoyed him most is Monteil's criticism that he, Mauger, should allow his servant, Rose, to share his table. In the light of this it is tempting to regard Mauger as an anti-bourgeois figure, echoing the rebellious Gaston Modot in L'Age d'Or and anticipating the liberal pronouncements of Don Lope in Tristana. That Mauger is an active, robust and vital man totally different from the ultra-refined Rabour is suggested throughout, while the impression is reinforced through the association with him - as he shatters Monteil's greenhouse - of the favourite Buñuelian motif of ants, symbolic of vigorous activity. When we see him cutting the branches of Monteil's trees and hurling them into his garden, we are reminded too of Buñuel's own aggression in 1931 when, at a Christmas party given by Charlie Chaplin in Hollywood, he and a group of fellow surrealists set about chopping down the Christmas tree, for them a symbol of bourgeois life.

In reality, despite impressions to the contrary, Mauger shows himself to be a true bourgeois. His unconventional association with his servant does not disguise his sense of honour, the conservatism to be expected of a retired army officer: 'The word of a soldier ... is certainly something ...!' (¡La palabra de un soldado ... es ciertamente algo ...!) (p. 100). When Monteil accuses him in the presence of a judge, Mauger defends his own good name and that of the army. But what, in the end, do Mauger's honour and standards of behaviour amount to? Firstly, fancying his chances with Célestine, this old Don Juan dismisses Rose, his servant and mistress of ten years' standing. The initially attractive rebel is thus, ultimately, as unsympathetic, as much a predator as Monteil himself. Moreover, by the end of the film Mauger and Monteil have not merely resolved their differences, but Mauger has even come to like his former enemy:

> Ah! Tomorrow morning I'll go hunting with Monteil. I have to admit he's a good chap ... [13]

The old rebel, married to the attractive Célestine and given to hunting with his next-door neighbour, has settled for a comfortable bourgeois life. Again we are reminded of Don Lope in Tristana. In one of the film's later scenes the old man who has earlier flaunted his liberal attitudes is seen at home in an atmosphere of cosy conventionality eating biscuits and drinking chocolate with his friends, the priests. Buñuel, for all his onslaughts on bourgeois life and attitudes, recognizes its insidious influence and its enormous powers of resistance.

Diary of a Chambermaid presents an upstairs-downstairs situation in which the servants both reflect and differ from their masters. Célestine is, of course, important in this respect, but let us first consider Joseph, perhaps the most intriguing character in the film, and certainly one of the best drawn in terms of Buñuel's insight into the deeper recesses of the human mind.

In many ways Joseph is entirely different from his bourgeois masters. Thus, his physically strong, robust, peasant physique and his terse and often silent manner contrast markedly with the refinement both of bourgeois dress and bourgeois speech:

> *Joseph, a peasant of about forty, with a broad forehead and short, thick hair. He has a taciturn appearance ... Joseph is a peasant with strong hands and gestures that are precise and few ...* [14]

In other respects, though, Joseph is a virtual mirror of his masters. Firstly, he is a fascist. In a sequence fairly early in the film he is seen reading a political newspaper and approving the action taken the previous night against certain groups of which he disapproves. Buñuel, as we have seen, has updated Mirbeau's novel to 1928 or thereabouts, thereby placing it in the context of political and nationalist unrest in Europe. In a conversation with the sacristan, Joseph vociferously expresses his anti-semitism, approving the fact that twelve Jews have been killed in Rumania:

> SACRISTAN (*with satisfaction*): And in Rumania they have killed twelve Jews!
> JOSEPH: Twelve fewer! That was certainly worth the effort! [15]

Anti-semitism, the sacristan observes to Marianne, is bound up with feelings of nationalism and patriotism, a view with which Joseph agrees. And he shares the sacristan's opinion that France's decline is occasioned by the fact that the Jews control both the Government and the Law. In the film's last sequence Buñuel focuses on a fascist demonstration, all the more frightening because of the jerky, leap-frogging way in which it is presented. The fascist banners reflect Joseph's sentiments and it is he who comes out from his café to watch the demonstration and to join in the shouting of the fascist slogans. The café is called, significantly, 'The French Army', a fact which links Joseph with Mauger, the retired army captain who also reveals anti-Jewish sentiments. In short,

Joseph, for all his peasant background, has much of the mentality of his bourgeois masters. The storm with which the film concludes is indicative of the forces which he and his kind will soon unleash in Europe.

Closely linked with Joseph's fascism are his cruelty and violence, exposed by Buñuel with masterly precision. They are revealed in the film in two episodes of a quite horrific nature. In the first Joseph is seen killing a goose, prolonging its agony with sadistic delight and deliberation. Buñuel provides us with a very effective close-up, accompanied by the creature's agonized cries and Joseph's callous words:

> Squawking of the goose.
> A close-up of the tormented goose, followed by another in which it beats its wings in desperation. They take up the whole screen ...
> JOSEPH (voice off-screen): Let them suffer, let them suffer! The more they suffer, the better they taste afterwards! [16]

Subsequently, in advance of the second episode, a link is established between the goose and Claire, the ragged orphan who wanders about the estate, for Joseph's hands are seen in close-up encircling the girl's neck. The clear and chilling implications of the incident are realized when Joseph violates and kills Claire - an episode which is left to our imagination but whose consequences Buñuel's camera reveals in the most matter-of-fact, documentary-like manner:

> A little further on there can be seen behind some scrub (the harsh whistle of a train in the distance) the leg of the little girl and a foot with a shabby shoe (the camera advances accompanied by the sound of the distant train). Claire is stretched on the ground, her legs apart; on one of them a bloodstain ... [17]

But while Buñuel exposes the violent, sadistic and murderous outbursts to which Joseph - and thus the fascist mentality - is given, he allows us to see too, with a rare and penetrating insight, the otherwise tidy, neat and punctilious façade behind which such a man conceals his taste for violence or within which he contains it. Thus, Joseph's room is tidily kept, as are the things in the cupboard in the room:

> Inside the cupboard everything is carefully arranged ...[18]

The camera reveals boots, shirts, socks, sweaters, handkerchiefs, newspapers, bottles, glasses and various other objects all set out in immaculate order. It is a tellingly observed, clinically accurate portrait of an over-anxious, obsessive neurotic, but there is also another angle to Buñuel's portrayal of the servant. His fastidiousness clearly relates him to his bourgeois masters; to Rabour with his neat album of pictures and his ladies' boots, carefully arranged in the cupboard; and to Madame Monteil with her china ornaments and her display cases immaculately kept throughout the house. In addition, the walls of Joseph's room are covered with objects - the tricolour, nationalistic and patriotic pictures and slogans, and religious images - which indicate that Joseph's preoccupations with country and Church are precisely those of his employers. In him their values, as well as their cruelty and secret perversions, are embodied in a more vigorous and active form. Buñuel's portrayal of this violent but fastidious man is one of the film's real triumphs.

What can we say, then, of Célestine, whose diary this is? She is undoubtedly given her distinctive qualities, one in a line of Buñuelian characters - Viridiana, Séverine, Tristana - whose experience is to do, in one way or another, with freedom, whether it be consciously pursued, as in Tristana's case, or achieved almost unwillingly and in the most unexpected way, as with Viridiana. As far as Célestine is concerned, the point is made from the outset that she is no ordinary, submissive servant. Indeed, there is about her a certain superiority, reflected in her dress. Her arrival at the small provincial town shows her to be dressed rather elegantly. The scenario reads:

> She is dressed with a certain elegance; she wears a hat and shoes of patent leather.[19]

Later, taking her on a guided tour of the house, Madame Monteil observes of Célestine's clothes:

> One can see that you come from Paris ... This type of dress is not suited to the countryside.[20]

There are occasions too, quite early in the film, when Célestine has no hesitation in pouring scorn on the family which now employs her. Madame Monteil has pointed out to her with an air of superiority that if a certain lamp is broken, it can be repaired only in England. In a subsequent conversation with the servants, Célestine comments:

> 'Take great care. If it is broken, we shall have to send it to England to be repaired.' (She turns to the other women and, reverting to her normal voice and not without a certain rather vulgar aggression, adds:) And if she breaks her piss-pot, does she send it to London too? (She pauses). I don't know if I can stand three days in this shack.[21]

At an early stage, then, Célestine asserts a kind of independence and on more than one occasion shows every sign of being a disruptive element in the bourgeois household.

She asserts her independence too in relation to the two men, Monteil and Rabour. Towards the amorous but ineffectual Monteil, Célestine consistently adopts a mocking stance, teasing and manipulating him at her leisure:

> Célestine leans on the table and answers him provocatively, as much through the tone of her voice as through her posture.[22]

When he grabs her waist, she reverts to a formal attitude, reminding him of his wife:

> He takes her by the waist. Célestine readopts a formal attitude and feigns surprise:
> CÉLESTINE: What, sir?
> MONTEIL: You know what I mean.
> CÉLESTINE (as though the thought had occurred to her only at that moment): Does my master want me to deceive my mistress with my master?[23]

In keeping Monteil on a string, Célestine preserves her freedom and integrity in more than merely sexual terms.

Towards Rabour, the undisputed master of the household, Célestine's behaviour is, of necessity, different. She thus agrees to his request that she wear the leather boots - an apparent surrender of her independence. On the other hand, it is soon apparent to Célestine that Rabour is much more interested in the boots than in the woman. He does not, like his son-in-law, represent a real sexual threat to her and she is able, without unduly compromising herself, to indulge what is little more than an eccentric whim on Rabour's part - and to indulge it with indifference, safely distancing herself from any real involvement. If her reaction to Monteil is provocative and mocking, she treats Rabour with a patient tolerance. On both counts Célestine emerges as an intelligent, astute girl who knows the way of the world and how to manipulate it to her own advantage.

It is Célestine's relationship with Joseph that, on account of its complexity and ambiguity, remains one of the film's most fascinating features. On the one hand, from the very moment when in the opening sequence he meets her at the station, Célestine dislikes Joseph intensely. He, a rough, taciturn and often crude individual, is her complete opposite. Later, she is particularly upset by his sadistic killing of the goose. The scenario reads:

> What she sees - but not the spectator - horrifies her (rapid shots of both of them). [24]

Immediately, she shouts to him:

> Quickly! Kill it at once! Don't make it suffer like that! [25]

In the following sequence, while the servants eat their evening meal, Célestine rejects Joseph's abrupt request for an apple and cuttingly accuses him of telling tales about her to Madame Monteil:

> I am not used to waiting on ... (with an even more scornful and somewhat crude emphasis:) ... telltales, understand? [26]

Throughout the meal the gulf between Célestine and Joseph is further emphasized by the fact that her sympathies lie with the little girl, Claire, whom Joseph delights in frightening and whom he will soon kill. When Claire grows tired, Célestine takes her to her room and puts her in her own bed. Moreover, while Célestine refuses to give Joseph an apple, she gives one to Claire. As far as the young girl is concerned, the apple, with its Biblical connotations, suggests innocence, and, inasmuch as Célestine is linked to Claire through the apple, it indicates that she too, though a mature and astute woman, is at least part of that innocence. We are reminded of the way in which, in Tristana, the young Tristana gives an apple to the deaf-mute, Saturno, and of how at the end of Nazarín a woman offers a pineapple to the suffering priest - both acts of generosity and human kindness. In Diary of a Chambermaid the point is that Joseph is excluded from such acts.

Joseph's murder of Claire - and Célestine always suspects him of it - intensifies Célestine's hostility towards him. From the moment of her first suspicions she is filled with rage, heightened by her affection for the young and innocent girl. Given this, we cannot doubt the fact that Célestine's closer involvement with Joseph stems from a desire firstly to extract the truth from him, and, having done so, to expose him as the murderer. Thus, in a sequence in Joseph's room when he sits beside her, the scenario underlines Célestine's feelings of antipathy:

> Célestine's posture remains the same. The repulsion which he awakens in her and the hatred which she feels towards him ... [27]

But it continues:

> ... begins to give way to that strange fascination which he holds for her from the moment when she suspects that he may be a murderer. [28]

In short, Célestine's reaction, initially hostile, is now ambivalent, a mixture of repulsion and attraction. The fascination which Joseph has for her cannot, of course, be explained logically. Buñuel has repeated time and time again that he is fascinated by the instinctive and the irrational and by the contradictions and ambiguities in human behaviour. Célestine's attraction to Joseph can be understood easily enough in that context. The knowledge that, before killing Claire, he has violated her awakens in Célestine the desire, strange and irresistible as it is, to be dominated sexually by this silent, brutal and violent man. In this respect a comparison can be made between Célestine and Séverine in Belle de Jour. In the opening sequence of that film Séverine dreams of sexual domination at the hands of her husband's servants. In the course of the film she is propelled by subconscious desires to transform dream into reality, which she does in effect by working in a brothel and, as far as a regular lover is concerned, by exchanging her elegant, well-mannered husband, Pierre, for the rough and aggressive young gangster, Marcel. Séverine's experience is one in which she escapes from the bourgeois chains of sexual guilt and inhibition to a new sexual and emotional freedom. Célestine's experience, granted that she is very different from Séverine, is in the same category, Joseph's influence on her a strange kind of liberation. It is certainly interesting to contrast the fascination which she feels for Joseph, a strong, physical type, with the indifference with which she regarded the over-refined Rabour. Why, then, if Joseph frees her in this way, does she denounce him to the police?

The answer to this question is really quite simple. Joseph, in discussing marriage with Célestine, reveals his plan to buy a restaurant in Cherbourg where she will prove a prime attraction for soldiers and sailors alike. Célestine immediately understands:

> In other words, you want me to work as a prostitute for you, right? [29]

Joseph can only reply:

> You shouldn't look at things like that. It's a business arrangement, nothing more ... [30]

The coldness evident in Joseph in so many ways distinguishes his attitude to marriage to Célestine. For him she would be merely a sexual object, to be used and abused according to his whims, no more important as an individual than she has been for Rabour or Monteil. If Joseph has in a sense liberated her sexual feelings, he offers her a marriage which denies her freedom. Realizing the implications, Célestine asserts her independence by denouncing Joseph to the police for Claire's murder, freeing herself of him once and for all.

The film ends with Célestine's marriage to Mauger, the eccentric next-door neighbour, as a result of which she leaves behind her servant status and becomes instead mistress of the household. Earlier in the film, prior to Joseph's proposal of marriage, Mauger has himself proposed to her, promising her freedom from household chores:

> We'll get someone in who'll be responsible for cooking ... [31]

After the marriage Célestine is seen eating her breakfast in bed, no longer waiting but being waited upon:

> ... Célestine is still in bed, the breakfast tray in front of her ... [32]

To all appearances Célestine's story is a success story. Availing herself of her ingenuity she has emerged unscathed from her experiences with her bourgeois employers and subsequently ditched the even more ominous Joseph. Mauger, moreover, for all his eccentricity, is not too bad a catch. Despite his age he is a vigorous and cheerful man and he accords Célestine due respect. On the other hand, it is soon perfectly clear that if Célestine has avoided numerous traps, she has merely walked into another. Mauger observes of her that she looks sad, a remark which at the beginning of the film Célestine has herself made of the countryside as she is driven to the bourgeois house. Speaking to her new husband, Célestine reveals a surprising indifference. The explanation lies in the fact that Mauger, the eccentric rebel who once amused her, has in the meantime undergone a transformation whereby he no longer abuses his neighbour, Monteil, but expresses admiration for him and joins him when he goes hunting. In the end, then, Mauger has become, as it were, a paid-up member of the bourgeoisie, another Monteil, and Célestine a bourgeois wife, a sexual object to be left at home or put on display as Mauger wishes. Her hoped-for liberty is to that extent an imprisonment in the bourgeois world from which till now she has been excluded and which, ironically in her acceptance of Mauger, she has agreed to join. Célestine is not yet Tristana, rejecting her old husband in a defiant assertion of her independence, but her future could well be that. What seems certain is that in the Mauger household she is already like one of those vases or pieces of furniture that adorn Madame Monteil's sitting-room - beautiful but dead.

In terms of its technique, Diary of a Chambermaid exemplifies many, if not all, of the characteristic features of Buñuel's cinematic style. Firstly, Buñuel's manner is in general simple, direct and unfussy, avoiding the showy camerawork of many directors. Jean-Claude Carrière, who has worked closely with Buñuel since 1963, has made the following observation:

> He steers clear of unusual angles or sophisticated camera work ... The solution is usually the simplest, or sometimes just the easiest ... Once he's satisfied with a take, he goes on to the next ... [33]

Buñuel, it should be remembered, worked for many years in the Mexican commercial cinema, forced by ridiculously low budgets and time-limits to make full-length films in a matter of weeks. Secondly, he has always been interested in making documentaries. Both these facts account for the matter-of-fact simplicity and speed of his films. Of Diary of a Chambermaid the Spanish critic, Francisco Aranda, comparing it with Renoir's version, has stated:

> Buñuel's adaptation is concise, and marvellously concise the use of image. Brusque cuts in the editing carry us rapidly from one scene to another ... [34]

The remark is very apt, for the film certainly moves with pace and precision. The effect of this, a characteristic feature of all Buñuel's films, is to eliminate that sentimental lingering over certain shots that is so obvious a device in many film directors. Instead, Buñuel presents things as he sees them, allowing situations to speak for themselves.

While the style of Diary is straightforward - some critics have said old-fashioned -, special attention should be paid to Buñuel's use of close-ups and their function within the film. Numerous examples present themselves; the various objects that adorn Madame Monteil's sitting-room; Rabour's album of postcards; the goose frantically flapping its wings; Joseph's hands around Claire's neck; Célestine walking across the room wearing the boots; the leg of the dead Claire; Célestine's face as she hears the news of Claire's death. If we consider a few of these examples, we can see that their purpose, far from being arbitrary, is quite precise. When, for instance, Buñuel gives us a close-up of the ornaments in Madame Monteil's sitting-room, he does so to show us the importance, the central role that they have in her life. In short, they are given the prominence in cinematic terms that they have for her in actuality. In addition, though, the close-up also allows us to draw a certain conclusion about Madame Monteil's values, for it enables us to see all the better that the objects which she prizes above all else are cold and inanimate things - a reflection, in short, of her own coldness. Another important aspect of the close-up in any Buñuel film is that it reveals and exposes instantly the workings of a character's mind, allowing us to see something as he or she sees it. For example, the close-up of the goose flapping its wings in agony evokes with great power and conciseness not merely the goose's torment but Joseph's sadistic delight in observing that torment, for we see it with his eyes. Similarly, when Célestine wobbles across the room in the leather boots, the close-up of the boots pinpoints Rabour's fixation, for the camera focuses on that area on which his own eyes are riveted. In short, close-up in the film becomes a guide to the mental and psychological processes of the characters, an instrument of surrealism.

Diary of a Chambermaid is notable amongst Buñuel's films for the absence of dream-sequences. In most of Buñuel's major films - Los olvidados, The Exterminating Angel, Belle de Jour, The Discreet Charm of the Bourgeoisie - the dreams, or even the day-dreams of the characters, reveal their inner lives, their longings, their preoccupations, their terrors. In certain cases, as in Belle de Jour, dreams or day-dreams are used extensively, to a point where they account for a very large part of the film. In other films, as in Tristana, dreams are used very sparingly, though that in itself adds to their power. And in some films - Viridiana, Diary of a Chambermaid - they do not occur at all. Here, as the previous paragraph has suggested, the inner lives of the characters are revealed to us through the prominence accorded, often in close-up, to certain objects. In Viridiana shots of feet, legs, a cow's udder, the handles of a skipping-rope, forge a network of motifs which allows us, as effectively as in dream-sequences, to gain access to the characters' unspoken thoughts. In Diary a similar chain of meaningful images is constructed: postcards, boots, feet, legs, faces, hands, animals, birds. Buñuel never photographs them for their own sake. His films have a language, a concise cinematic language which, looked at in the context of the film as a whole, hangs together beautifully.

In conclusion, it is evident that in terms of themes and technique _Diary of a Chambermaid_ is a highly representative film. More than that, though, it seems to me a very good film. Its reputation has suffered unduly, no doubt, on account of the films that preceded and succeeded it - _Viridiana_, _The Exterminating Angel_, _Belle de Jour_. In most respects, as the preceding analysis suggests, _Diary_ matches up to them.

GWYNNE EDWARDS

University College of Wales
Aberystwyth

NOTES

1 For general studies of Buñuel's films see Freddy Buache, The Cinema of Luis Buñuel, trans. Peter Graham (London and New York, 1973); Raymond Durgnat, Luis Buñuel (London, 1967); Virginia Higginbotham, Luis Buñuel (Boston, 1979); Ado Kyrou, Luis Buñuel (Paris, 1962); Joan Mellen (ed.), The World of Luis Buñuel: Essays in Criticism (New York, 1978); Francisco Aranda, Luis Buñuel: A Critical Biography, trans. David Robinson (London, 1975); Gwynne Edwards, The Discreet Art of Luis Buñuel (London and Boston, 1982).

2 The reference is to the film scenario in the series Colección Voz Imagen (Barcelona, 1971).

3 Tom Milne, 'The Two Chambermaids', in Joan Mellen (ed.), The World of Luis Buñuel, 260. The essay first appeared in Sight and Sound, 33 (1964).

4 Tom Milne, art. cit., 260.

5 Freddy Buache, op. cit., 143; Tom Milne, art. cit., 265.

6 Freddy Buache, op. cit., 151.

7 All translations into English are my own and are based on the Spanish version of the film scenario published in the series Colección Voz Imagen (Barcelona, 1963).
Ya en el gran salón, la señora Monteil se dirige hacia una cómoda sobre la cual pueden verse diferentes chucherías. Plano muy próxima para mostrarnosla en detalle: dos figuritas de porcelana y una tabaquera de concha y plata (22).

8 Las dos mujeres llegan al extremo del pequeño salón, donde se abre el dintel que comunica con el gran salón. Sin una palabra de explicación, la señora Monteil se descalza. Célestine la contempla, sorprendida (21).

9 ... sobre la cual [la cama] aparece el señor Rabour tendido, con las sábanas en desorden cubriendo parcialmente su desnudez. Todavía sostiene en su mano uno de los botines. El señor Rabour está muerto (83).

10 'Viniendo del jardín, siempre se trae algo de tierra en los zapatos ...' (22).

11 En el gran salón, la señora Monteil está ocupada en la casi ritual limpieza de los delicados y preciosos objetos que hay en la estancia. Está junto a la vitrina, con una gamuza en la mano. No lleva zapatos, para no ensuciar la alfombra (124).

12 El señor Monteil es un hombre de unos cuarenta años de edad. Es alto y fuerte, un tanto sanguíneo. Su rostro denota falta de voluntad y, sobre todo, de inteligencia. No tiene ninguna

importancia ni peso en la casa, donde todo pertenece a su suegro. Es un perfecto ocioso (27).

13 '¡Ah! Mañana por la mañana iré de caza con Monteil. Debo reconocerlo: es un buen hombre ...' (142).

14 Joseph, campesino de unos cuarenta años de edad, de frente estrecha y cabellos cortos y abundantes. Con aspecto taciturno ... Joseph es un campesino de manos fuertes y gestos precisos y parcos ... (16).

15 SACRISTÁN (complacidamente): Y, en Rumania, han matado a doce judíos.
JOSEPH: ¡Doce menos! Esto es algo que ha valido la pena, ¿no? (56).

16 Graznidos de la oca.
Primerísimo plano de la oca agonizante, seguido de otro batiendo desesperadamente las alas, que ocupan por completo la pantalla ...
JOSEPH (voz en off): ¡Que sufran, que sufran! ¡Cuanto más sufren, mejor saben luego! (49).

17 Algo más lejos, puede distinguirse, detrás de un matorral (silbido estridente de un tren que corre a lo lejos), la pierna de la niña con un pie pobremente calzada (travelling hacia adelante acompañado del ruido del paso lejano de un tren). Claire está tendida en el suelo, con las piernas abiertas; en una aparecen manchas de sangre ... (85).

18 En el interior del armario todo está cuidadosamente dispuesto ... (108).

19 Va vestida con cierta elegancia; sombrero y zapatos de charol (15).

20 'Se ve que viene usted de París ... Esta clase de vestido no está hecha para el campo' (23).

21 'Tenga usted mucho cuidado. Si se estropea, deberíamos enviarla a Inglaterra para su reparación'. (Se vuelve hacia las otras mujeres y, recobrando su voz natural y no sin cierta agresividad un tanto vulgar, añado:) Y su orinal, cuando se raja, ¿lo envía también a Londres? (Una pausa). No sé si podré aguantar tres días en esta barraca (31).

22 Célestine se apoya en la mesa y responde provocadoramente tanto con el tono de la voz como con la actitud (46).

23 La coge por la cintura. Célestine recupera su aspecto formal y finge sorpresa:

CÉLESTINE: ¿Qué, señor?
MONTEIL: Usted ya lo sabe.
CÉLESTINE (como si sólo se le ocurriera pensarlo en aquel instante); ¿El señor quisiera que yo enganase a la señora con el señor? (47).

24 Lo que ella ve - pero no el espectador - la horroriza (planos breves de una y otro) (49).

25 '¡Pero, vamos! ¡Mátela en seguida! ¡No la haga sufrir así!' (49).

26 'No estoy acostumbrada a servir ... (*con acento todavía más despreciativo, incluso un tanto vulgar*:) ... a los soplones, ¿sabe?' (54-55).

27 *La actitud de Célestine no varía. La repulsión que le inspira y el odio que siente hacia él* ... (111).

28 ... *van cediendo lugar a esa extraña fascinación que él ejerce sobre ella desde que sospecha que pueda ser un homicida* (111).

29 'En otras palabras, usted quisiera que haga de puta por usted, ¿no?' (121).

30 'No debe mirar las cosas de esa manera. Es un negocio, nada más ...' (121).

31 'Ya tendremos a alguien que se encargue de cocinar ...' (117).

32 ... *Célestine, todavía acostada, con la bandeja del desayuno ante ella* ... (141).

33 'The Buñuel Mystery', in Joan Mellen (ed.), *The World of Luis Buñuel*, 93-94. The article first appeared in *Show* (1970).

34 *Luis Buñuel: A Critical Biography*, 220.

LUIS BUÑUEL: OBJECTS AND PHANTOMS

The Montage of *Viridiana*

It is axiomatic to say that the art of a master craftsman lies in his knack of exploiting the properties inherent in his medium, but when the medium is film and the craftsman Luis Buñuel it is sometimes necessary to state the obvious. Buñuel, it seems to me, and as I wish to show in connexion with the film *Viridiana*, offers a fine example of an art based on the highlighting of a medium's special and intrinsic attributes.

Let us begin by isolating two attributes of film which might be considered primary. First, its objectivity or plasticity calls attention; as a celluloid record of what is or once was there, film has a remarkable facility for reproducing the objects, big and small, of reality itself. Second, and quite the opposite, the phantasmagoric and dreamlike quality of film is equally renowned; the kinetic form of what is sometimes called the motion picture has a supreme capacity, when aided by devices of montage, to produce a shifting succession and medley of images relevant to the inner mind, to dream, the imagination, fantasy. It might be said that these two facilities mark the extreme boundaries of the film-maker's domain, Buñuel's included to judge from his first three films which were, precisely, cinepoems in *An Andalusian Dog* (1928) and *The Golden Age* (1930), and a brutal documentary in *Land Without Bread* (1932). Certainly these two distinctive and apparently antithetical aspects of film - reality and dream, objects and phantoms - demand close attention in any appreciation of Buñuel's art.

Naturally a film-maker is not obliged to choose between these facilities as though having just two lenses with which to mount his camera, the one so transparent it lets reality stream through with less fuss than any realist prose, the other a prodigious image-making prism and the envy of the most fertile poet. But such alternativeness did apply and was even necessary in the early days of cinema when the issue of film as an art form was contentious to say the least, dismissed and ridiculed by die-hard elder statesmen like Unamuno in Spain, hailed as the 'seventh art' by young partisans like Buñuel.[1] In that climate it was only natural than an earnest film-maker would wish to show off his new medium, exaggerating its artistic attributes both to distinguish it from the commercial Hollywood cinema and to outgun the noble genres at their own game. Other reasons too would have encouraged Buñuel to proselytise the cinema in extreme form. The impact of Freudian psychology was, as we know, decisive as regards those avant-gardists Buñuel knew as friends at the Student Residence in Madrid in the early twenties, García Lorca, Rafael Alberti and Salvador Dalí among them. The paramountcy of the image as an expression of the unconscious was confirmed by the Surrealists whom Buñuel joined in Paris in the late twenties. But there, in Breton, Aragon and the others, Buñuel also found a different kind of commitment, one born of the political fervour of the times and much concerned with everyday material reality. This was Communism, which, though not attracting Buñuel for a great length of time, nonetheless left its mark, as Land Without Bread testifies. Looking back on Buñuel's long career it is plain that he surrendered neither the realism nor the fantasy of film; he remained a prolific image-maker while at the same time his interest in the object-littered world in which people live - either as complacent bourgeois or as _pícaros_ of the ghetto - never diminished. But what I suggest did happen in the course of time is that the polarisation and alternativeness between reality and dream ceased to apply, or at least it came to apply only in subtle form. Buñuel found it was no longer necessary to go to Las Hurdes, that most deprived part of Spain, to shoot reality, and likewise he found ways of introducing images in films other than cinepoems. The outstanding achievement of Buñuel's art, it seems to me, is that not only does he film reality and dream through the same lens but he manages to synthesise the two worlds so completely that one might say he films objects and phantoms at the same time, in the same shot.

That the two worlds of reality and dream should meet was inevitable in Buñuel from a thematic point of view, given that his preoccupation is always _freedom_. On the one hand, it goes without saying that to depict the real situation in which people live is to depict the impositions placed upon individual liberty by the forces of society, by 'the so-called pillars of society', as Buñuel sarcastically puts it, 'our most unjust social institutions, like religion, the fatherland, the family, culture'. [2] In all his films the individual strives not to be dashed against one or other of these pillars, pillars which in fact Buñuel frequently films in all their concrete splendour. On the other hand, as regards images, it is no less clear that fantasy is the individual's psychic expression of freedom, of his aspiration towards a kind of freedom which in all probability will be denied. Often the images of fantasy are linked by nothing more than what is known as 'free association', which is to say, somewhat problematically, connexions made by and peculiar to the mind of a certain individual acting with apparent freedom. Ultimately the linking of more or less incongruous images - a practice of the Surrealists and of the early Buñuel - is a way of celebrating what is idiosyncratic in an individual, and the cult of the incongruous is the cult of freedom.

Linked to the idea of free association is the key notion of transformation, that is, the capacity of any image or thing to transform itself - thanks to the liberating power of the imagination - into something else. This notion is prominent in much twentieth-century literature, notably in two poets well known to Buñuel personally, García Lorca and Octavio Paz, who illustrate the point in separate ways. In the more pessimistic Lorca, transformation reflects the individual's need to break out of the prison of his own identity, as for instance in the cinematic skit, Buster Keaton's Walk, where the tragic Keaton sighs:

> I would like to be a swan. But I can't, though
> I would like to. For where would I leave my hat?
> And where my collar and moiré tie? What a pity! [3]

Here we see that objects or things, the very trappings of reality, hat, tie and so on, frustrate Keaton's dream of liberation, his wish to be a swan. In another piece, 'Introduction to Death' from Poet in New York, Lorca simply lists the transformational desires of animals:

> What an effort!
> What an effort from the horse to be a dog!
> What an effort from the dog to be a swallow!
> What an effort from the swallow to be a bee!
> What an effort from the bee to be a horse!
> ... And me, along the gables,
> what a cherub of flames do I seek and be! [4]

The childish tone here and in the Keaton piece is not uncommon in Lorca, a poet who delighted in lullabies and children's songs, no doubt because children have a great talent for transforming reality in their games. But for Lorca this remains the prerogative of the child, while the adult aspires towards a transformation that is unrealisable. In the modern Mexican poet Octavio Paz, on the other hand, who was himself much influenced by Surrealism, we see the positive side of transformation. In his magical poem 'Sun Stone', composed of nearly six hundred lines without a single full stop, it seems that everything has the power to change itself - to transfigure itself, as he puts it - into something else, and man likewise frees himself:

> trapdoors, cells, enchanted caves,
> birdcages and numbered rooms,
> all are transfigured, all fly,
> each moulding is a cloud, each door
> looks onto the sea, fields, air, each table
> is a banquet ...
> everything transfigures itself and is sacred ...[5]

This Buddhist rather than Christian sense of oneness makes the point that man can attain freedom if he realises that creation is a vast, mobile and interchanging reality of which man is himself a kinetic part. It might be added that the execution of the poem is much indebted to cinematic technique, for its sentenceless structure which allows image after image and object after object to blend into one another is as fluid as film rather than compartmentalised in the manner of punctuated language.

The bearing of this on Buñuel is both general and specific, and indeed the film maker combines Paz's kind of transformational vitality with Lorquian pessimism. In broad terms it is my point to stress that the very nature of the film medium is perfectly suited to the exploration of the inner mind even when all it films is exterior reality. The cuts, fades, juxta- and trans-positions which make up the repertoire of montage show us reality in a totally fluid and ever changing state, that is, reality as it seems to the inner mind. But although this transformational power of film is fully exploited by Buñuel, to the extent that it may even suggest the individual's inveterate desire for freedom, the objects which are transformed under the eye of his camera frequently carry with them reverse implications which deny that freedom. An example of such an object in Viridiana is the skipping-rope which we may consider in some detail since it is perhaps the most expressive object in the film and appears so often as to form a leitmotif.

Initially, when the young girl Rita uses the rope to skip, it is of innocuous value, a toy, an association with childhood innocence. But naturally this connects with Viridiana herself, the novice nun, whose desire for purity and innocence is captured on the occasion when she joins in with Rita's skipping game. In the meantime we see that Viridiana's uncle, Don Jaime, is more than a little entertained by watching young Rita skip - 'He makes me skip' (44),[6] she says - and the camera's focus on her jumping legs is ominous. Presently Don Jaime, ashamed at having taken advantage of Viridiana by drugging her, hangs himself with the same skipping-rope and from the very tree under which Rita always skipped, and the connexion between the object and sexuality becomes plain. This is soon highlighted when one of Viridiana's beggars discovers the rope and uses it around his waist as a belt. Finally, when this beggar attempts to rape Viridiana, a touch of the patently phallic handle of the skipping-rope is enough to make her pass out. In short, we see that the rope has not only represented Viridiana's longing for purity, her most cherished dream, but also her nightmarish fears of sexuality. So far, however, the transformations from toy to noose to phallic symbol are of a kind which arguably any other medium might achieve. To find the full cinematic sense of transformation we need to look closely at the montage with its repeated focus and sometimes steady close-up on the skipping-rope which pinpoint its values. There is one notable occasion when it is closely juxtaposed with a scene in which Viridiana is hesitant of milking a cow. She is invited to perform this simple country chore by a farm-hand - 'You have to pull very hard' (47), he instructs - and she is urged on by Rita who shouts 'Grip it tight!', adding with unwitting intent, 'Don Jaime is very good at it'. Viridiana's white hands are then seen tentatively approaching the cow's fleshy udders, but at the first touch she breaks away stammering, 'I don't know how to ... I can't ... it makes me feel very ...' (48). And although Viridiana is unable to explain her aversion, the relevance of this scene to her sexual make-up is clarified, perhaps again unknowingly, by Rita who immediately says she saw Viridiana undressing in her room the previous night, thereby doubling the nun's embarrassment. Visually, of course, the udders make an emphatic connexion with the handles of the skipping-rope which we have recently seen, and the whole sequence of the milking anticipates Viridiana's traumatic touching of the handle at the point of rape.

The rope image also illustrates specific attitudes of Buñuel which are comparable with Lorca's pessimism. The rope, as distinct from its handles, comes to assume a virtually separate value in the course of the film: that of bondage. The key to this is Don Jaime's suicide, with the powerful shot of him hanging by the rope from a stout tree being a clear sign of his admission of guilt, a consequence of being literally bound and tied to his baser instincts. The theme of bondage is echoed plentifully. The outcast beggar, El Leproso, is made to walk with a tin can tied to his waist by a string, a means of alerting the other beggars to his unwholesome presence (102). Here the connexion with eroticism is spelt out by the beggar who, denying that his offensive warts are leprous, explains how he contacted venereal disease from a bad woman one windy day. Viridiana, in the biblical fashion, kneels to untie his string, but events prove that her efforts to liberate him - whether from his ailment or his role as outcast - are futile. Bondage, together with the futility of freeing a subject from bondage, had been the point of an exemplary sequence not long before this when Jorge, the illegitimate son of Don Jaime, took pity on a dog mercilessly leashed between the wheels of a horse-drawn cart. Having bought the dog from its peasant owner, Jorge turns away with some sentimental satisfaction and fails to see a second identical cart making its way down the road with another dog running at a tight leash in what is evidently the local custom (100). Near the end of the film Jorge will himself be tied up with curtain cords by El Leproso. Less obvious echoes of the leash motif are also found, sometimes being no more than a backdrop to a shot: the servant Moncho leads his horse by the rein and, seeing Rita play with the rope by which his master hanged himself, snatches it from her and throws it into a field (75). The beggarwoman Enedina hangs clothes on a washing-line, a chore which, like her other duties as a mother of an infant, she finds onerous. Here the line is a succinct sign of the impositions made upon her freedom, not to say of the price she has to pay for undoubtedly licentious behaviour in the past. Similarly, Viridiana's settling down with a needle and thread at the end of the film (134) is a sign of her decision to submit to the domestic role of a normal woman, which means, in this context, being servile to the male and bound to his will. More elusive echoes may be briefly noted: Moncho repairs a leather strap (62); Jorge plays with the <u>cuerda</u> (literally 'cord' in Spanish, but here 'spring') of an old clock (106); Rita wears a strapped bandage around her head when she has toothache (113); the blind beggar's feet are entwined and bound by the bridal veil when he tries to escape the devastation of the banquet room (129); much to Don Jaime's admiration, Viridiana cuts an orange peel into a long strip which hangs from her hands in a rope-like spiral (57). In these ways Buñuel points up the visual motif of the rope, line, thread or leash, allowing the central object of the skipping-rope to reverberate through the film in a series of more or less recognisable transformations, the majority of which amplify the theme of bondage with some sexual reference.

The skipping-rope is thus an important integrational factor in Viridiana, attracting a cluster of parallel objects which help create a coherent visual rhythm in the film. It is a fine example of Buñuel's method of exteriorising inner thoughts, fantasies and even nightmares, that is, of presenting phantoms through objects. Given that his cinema can achieve this kind of articulation, it would seem strictly unnecessary to film the dreams themselves. By which yardstick Séverine's masochistic dream in Belle de Jour is a rare lapse by the craftsman, being somewhat redundant cinematically. It might be contrasted, for instance, with the way a rapacious sexual encounter is objectively caught in Tristana by the device of cutting abruptly from the bedroom scene to a violent charge of mounted Civil Guards upon defenceless workmen, a most telling and cinematic juxtaposition.[7] In any event it will be clear that the art of articulating through objects is very largely dependent upon the meaningfulness of the objects used, and here, it seems to me, Buñuel is much more at home when his subject is Spanish. In a Spanish context he is able to draw on a very rich tradition of objective symbolism. The deeply ingrained religious symbolism of Spain with its eschatological emphasis immediately comes to mind, and certainly Buñuel takes every advantage of its accoutrement, as in Viridiana's personal suitcase containing a crown of thorns, a wooden crucifix, nails, hammer and sponge (46). But in addition to this Spain has a very strong oral culture, or subculture, which is apt to express itself in highly visual and objective terms and which makes ideal cinematic material. There are proverbs, such as the one which forms the visual nucleus of Tristana, 'If you want an honest woman, break her leg and keep her at home',[8] which the film develops by having Tristana's leg amputated. There is also a strong tradition of popular symbolism, which may be illustrated by referring back to the orange which, as we saw a moment ago, Viridiana peeled for her uncle Don Jaime. To a Spanish audience it would be instantly understood that by this action Viridiana was demonstrating affection for the man. The complex of citrus symbolism, especially the contrast between the sweet orange and the bitter lemon, is one deeply rooted in the Spanish mentality, as numerous songs testify. The following, which is at least five hundred years old, gives some indication of the joy associated with the orange and of how the giving and receiving of an orange is a token of love:

> She threw me little oranges,
> with bunches of white orange blossom,
> she threw them to me and I to her,
> and she threw them back again to me.[9]

It is true that Don Jaime misconstrues or exaggerates Viridiana's affection, but the objective sign of the orange helps us understand and even partly mitigates his proposal of marriage that same evening. On the topic of popular song it is also worth pointing out that one of its most frequent themes traditionally is that of the nun, especially the novice nun. Various reasons, good and bad, are explored as to why a young girl should want to enter orders; one of the more negative reasons is fear, which, though put bluntly in the following ancient fragment, may, as we have already suggested, be part of Viridiana's make-up:

> As a young nun in religion
> do I wish to enter,
> so as not to be unhappily married.[10]

My main point here, however, is to suggest that Buñuel's system of articulation through objects is more pronounced in his Spanish and Spanish-American films, partly no doubt because he is instinctively attuned to that culture and partly because it is a culture which lends itself more readily. In his later French films objects seem to be used primarily to point up the possessive materialism of the bourgeoisie, or else the objects are so typically those of modern day mass-production that they merely suggest the emptiness of values, their main function as objects often being reduced to that of props for gags. In contrast Buñuel's two Spanish films, Viridiana and Tristana, have a far greater sense of period and tradition, and they are literally teeming with significant or thematic objects, as we have already partly seen in connexion with Viridiana. We might now turn to the film as a piece, paying special attention to the way Buñuel's cutting and arrangement of sequences - his montage - helps invest what is seen with meaning.

Viridiana was filmed in 1961 at Madrid studios and a country estate of the Marquis of Usia known as La Moraleja, not far from the capital. Shooting began on February 4th and, as is customary with Buñuel, progress was swift, the film being completed in time for the Cannes Festival in early May where it won the 'Palme d'or', the first Spanish film ever to win such a prestigious prize. In all it had cost little more than £30,000 to make, an astoundingly small sum. It was the first film Buñuel had made in Spain since Land Without Bread and indeed it was the first time he had returned home since the Civil War, a point which may partly account for the intensely Spanish and even nostalgic atmosphere of the film.

Viridiana was conceived and its scenario written before Buñuel left Mexico City for Madrid in November 1960. Its gestation period had in fact been very long for Buñuel tells us that it was based upon a dream he had at the age of fourteen about a woman being drugged and abused, while the name Viridiana is that of a little-known medieval saint he had heard of as a youth in Zaragoza.[11] Certainly this unusual name is apt, inviting speculation on the notions of virgen/virtud (virgin/virtue) and the goddess of chastity, Diana. But the salient point is that the narrative line is original to Buñuel, for while the majority of his films are based on literary works, which thus require the cutting of novelistic and uncinematic elements, in Viridiana we have, as it were, a film conceived as a film from the beginning. This may well explain why its structure is so stunningly simple and effective. Its running time of ninety minutes divides quite cleanly into three parts of nearly equal length. The first comprises sequences 1 to 75, a virtually self-contained narrative dealing with Viridiana's visit to her uncle's run-down estate. In the course of four days and three nights which are apparently consecutive the traumatic events occur which culminate in Don Jaime hanging himself. The second part, sequences 76 to 136, takes place a few days later, for Don Jaime has now been buried and his illegitimate son Jorge has come to claim his share of the inheritance. This part foregrounds Viridiana's new vocation, the turning of the estate into a charitable home for beggars, though it also pointedly sets her idealism against Jorge's practical plans to make the estate pay. Covering three days and nights, this second part is more anecdotal in that it involves character sketches of the various beggars, of Jorge and his unhappy mistress Lucía, as well as illustrations of Viridiana's many difficulties. The third and last part of the film runs from sequence 137 when the beggars are left unsupervised in the grand old house. As the day moves from afternoon well into the night, the increasingly debauched and reckless behaviour of the beggars ends in a veritable saturnalia at the banquet table. Surprised by the return of Jorge and Viridiana, there ensues a crescendo of violence and attempted rape which terminates with the arrival of the police in sequence 185. The last few shots, up to 195, are in the manner of a quiet epilogue, depicting the now disillusioned Viridiana's decision to be a normal earthbound woman, presumably Jorge's woman. The essential structure of the film, then, is that of three well balanced parts, which one is tempted to describe as 'movements' for their very different yet homogeneous mood and tempo. Notable is the way that the second part - with its sketches and thematic exempla, such as that of the leashed dog - separates and functions as a counterpoint to the two more forceful narrative sequences at the beginning and end, sequences which themselves are paralleled in the climactic near-rape of Viridiana in both cases.

To compare the film's structure with a musical score, such as the allegro-lento-allegro pattern of a concerto, is not as fanciful as it may seem, for indeed music is an integral feature of the film and consistently functions with thematic purpose. In the first part Don Jaime's affection for classical music is dwelt upon and a striking example of Buñuel's skills of montage is found in shots 5 to 9 which flash quickly from Don Jaime playing his harmonium in the dead of night to Viridiana undressing in her spartan room. The connexion between the scenes is strengthened by the camera focusing alternately on Don Jaime's feet upon the pedals and Viridiana's lower part as she peels off her stockings. When Don Jaime enters a state of ecstasy we are left to wonder if this is prompted solely by the music or by other less sublime thoughts, and the corollary of this may occur to the more cynical observer, that Viridiana's own ecstatic rite in front of the violent implements of the crucifixion is perhaps not entirely otherworldly. The following night Don Jaime plays Beethoven's 'Hymn to Joy' on his gramophone as he rapturously inspects his dead wife's bridal outfit (51), a choral piece which links well with Mozart's 'Requiem' played the next night when he abuses Viridiana in his necrophilic passion (61). It links too with the film's main musical theme, Handel's 'Messiah', which is heard during the credits at the beginning and when it comes thundering out from the gramophone in shots 157 to 178 as the beggars' orgy reaches new depths of depravity. As will readily be seen, the music is an ironic counterpoint to the visual content, suggesting a celebration of the world and the flesh in place of the composer's intended spiritual sublimation. It is no coincidence that the most intense and sustained musical sequences occur on those two separate occasions when Viridiana is abused, while the less tense middle section of the film is appropriately without music, save for Jorge's discordant attempt at the harmonium which offends the servant Ramona (81). A last musical point is made right at the end when jazz comes from the gramophone in Jorge's room where Viridiana is heading, capturing the sense of seduction and the easy if somewhat meaningless pleasure which now awaits the erstwhile nun. Jazz contrasts poignantly with the grandeur of the earlier classical pieces as well as with the sombre sound of tolling bells which once were heard (107). But what is noticeable about the various ways music is introduced in the film is the simple fact of its objective presence; it is played by the harmonium, the gramophone, the bells, and is thus always a real part of the action and the characters' experience, there being no background music as such. It functions, then, as a support for the transformation of objective reality into the world of dreams and phantoms, even if, as a counterpoint, it ultimately suggests that dreams, in the sense of idealism, are unrealisable.

The division into three clear parts, supported as it is by musical emphasis, gives a rhythmic structure to the film as a piece. It is also a highly functional kind of structure which recalls the precepts laid down by that patriarch of Spanish drama, Lope de Vega, who advocated the use of three acts: the first to state the argument, the second to complicate the situation, and the third to build up to a climax complete with dénouement. Buñuel may have come to appreciate the practical virtues of this system when he worked with Lorca on traditional Spanish plays at the Student Residence in Madrid. In any event it is clear that his film plants the dilemma of spirituality vis-à-vis worldliness very firmly in its first part, develops the contrast with the arrival of the beggars and the materialist Jorge in the second, and works through a fever pitch of biblical and bacchanalian cross-references in the third, until, at the very end, as Lope recommended, we discover which route Viridiana takes. Even then it is much in the traditional spirit of Spanish drama that we are left to wonder if Viridiana's decision to go to Jorge is a free one or one imposed upon her by events, so that the theological conundrum of destiny and free-will remains unresolved.

The clean structuring of the film in its grander perspective is equally apparent in its finer points of montage. In the first part, which culminates in Don Jaime's hanging, there are several elements which initiate a fine rhythmic flow. Of these the most immediately distinctive is the continual fluid change from day to night and back again to day. Much as it does increase our sense of narrative, this is more than a matter of consecutivity, for the main function of these transitions is to suggest objectively the different levels of consciousness. We are led repeatedly from the open, public world of day to the shadowy and clandestine night-world of inner thoughts. This is complemented by a spatial rhythm which fluctuates from external to internal shots, from the neglected grounds of the estate to the once splendid rooms of the house, a system which again leads from public areas to spatial retreats where Don Jaime and Viridiana in particular observe their respective rites in the utmost secrecy, save for the occasional spy. These two rhythms - day to night, outside to inside - emphasise the idea of withdrawal, while the secrecy attached to the dark inner world suggests something unwholesome. Here we find a residual influence of the Marquis de Sade, that philosopher of libertinism esteemed by the Parisian Surrealists and whose outlawed works Buñuel made every effort to obtain and read. [12] Don Jaime's estate is a version - much toned down, it is true - of the Sadian château or castle to which the libertine withdraws to practise vice safe from the punitive attempts of the world. Likewise Don Jaime is not a full-blown Sadian sodomist - a role Buñuel mischievously gave to a Christ-figure in The Golden Age - but his mentality and situation bear comparison. Essentially, as Roland Barthes showed in his study of Sade, [13] the ingredients of the Sadian situation are, firstly, withdrawal (possible only for those of superior class who can buy privacy to act out depravities upon young innocents in a master-slave context), and secondly, a meticulously planned approach to vice (the libertine constructs his perverse utopia by paying scrupulous attention to details of clothing, diet, drugs and any object or thing which leads to the consummation of his pleasure). Much in this spirit, Don Jaime is found alone with his utopian objects, the bridal outfit complete with veil, satin slippers, silk stockings, a corset and the traditional orange blossom, which, unlike the real orange Viridiana peels for him, is artificial and in any case was probably never given him by his wife who so mysteriously died on her wedding night. Far from being dead or lifeless, these are erogenous objects redolent with sensuality whose touch and smell transport Don Jaime into a voluptuous spasm of transvestism. Having made a complete inventory of them and having witnessed Viridiana sleepwalking, Don Jaime then plans the consummation of his desire for the following evening. This entails the sporting dressing-up of Viridiana in full bridal gown, holding a burning candelabra, her flowing train obligingly held by the slave-servant Ramona. Approximating to what Barthes calls the 'counter-striptease' in Sade, this occultation is highly sensuous, for the libertine's pleasure depends as much upon the objects as upon the person and will be had in the removal of all this paraphernalia.

The scenario tells us that Viridiana is both disgusted and amused (61) by this 'masquerade' which she acts out for her uncle's benefit. In view of what follows, her amusement reflects her naïveté, a primal requisite in the victim of any roué. As a bride she plays a child's make-believe game, but the role is one in keeping with her submissive nature and it echoes the master-slave principle of libertinism. The camera focuses upon her as she walks like a bride to the altar, Don Jaime ogling her all the while. Her slow, tentative walk, with her body upright and rigid except for the movement of her hidden legs, is of irresistible appeal to Don Jaime, as Buñuel has carefully prepared us to appreciate. Don Jaime's earlier delight in making the young Rita skip, his troubled pleasure on seeing Viridiana's carelessly exposed thigh during her sleepwalking trance, these are scenes which anticipate the now secretive pleasure of occultation. Indeed Buñuel has focused on legs since the film's opening shot which showed Viridiana walking with the Mother Superior, stopping occasionally to talk, then walking on again. Specific focus on legs had occurred in no less than eleven sequences before the bridal walk, it being something of a fetish in this among many of his films. But besides the simple fact of foregrounding an erotic motif, this device has other far-reaching implications. Essentially what the camera does by focusing in this way is to fragment the female body and it thus offers a kind of visual surgery and meticulous analysis of a bodily part which has been selected from the entire inventory of the body for special ravishment. Fragmentation has the effect of dehumanising the person involved, treating her as an erotic composite with various pleasure-giving sites or locations, with the result that the selected part becomes virtually the equivalent of an object. When, with the assistance of his paid accomplice Ramona, Don Jaime drugs Viridiana, he is poised to fulfil his design step by step and ravish both her items of clothing and her bodily items with indiscriminate pleasure. He recoils finally, it is true, and renounces his Sadian scheme after having taken only part stock of his prey, for unlike the libertine proper he has a moral conscience which will make him pay dearly. An exact final touch to the episode is given when Don Jaime, having seen Viridiana depart and having no doubt firmly set his mind on suicide, takes time in what is presumably his last act on earth to inspect his work-table, when, to quote the scenario, he 'meticulously places all his instruments in order' (73).

The abuse of Viridiana is related to great visual effect by Buñuel's system of fluctuating from interior to exterior shots. The crucial events within the house are witnessed by the girl Rita outside who first observes from the terrace and later climbs the fatal tree for a better vantage point. Since Rita has been closely linked with Viridiana - skipping with her and, as the scenario notes, wearing a shawl in the same manner (62) - her presence as witness to Viridiana's misfortune serves to increase the sense of violence done to a young, defenceless innocent. But it is the visual content which gains most from the shifting of perspective to the outside. From there the lit windows of the house burn luminously in the darkness, and this links well with the motif of the candelabra (58) and particularly with the flames of the fire which had earlier held hypnotic power over Viridiana (57). The first close-up of the fire and flames occurred immediately before Viridiana's sleepwalking, a sequence which ended in the grand gesture of the nun tipping ashes on Don Jaime's bed (53). No less an explicit sign of rejection and renunciation is found at the end when Viridiana's crown of thorns is thrown onto a bonfire where it burns in a bright circle (136). The fire is thus another motif thoroughly interwoven in the film, but perhaps its most telling form is that of the burning windows seen from the exterior during Don Jaime's aberration and again during the beggars' orgy when it is suggestive of uncontrollable passion and hell-fire.

It is also typical of Buñuel to cut rapidly, shifting five times on this occasion from Don Jaime inside to Rita outside. His natural preference for momentum rather than long scenes works well here, for had the fondling of Viridiana been overdone it might well have seemed distasteful or banal, while it is clear that the urgency of the cutting is an effective way of expressing Don Jaime's feverish mood and even his confusion. Rapid cutting will also serve Buñuel in the second part of the film where the group animation of the beggars is caught. But a further thematic function of montage emerges here. Its most consistent feature is juxtaposition, whereby Buñuel seeks to contrast the pious idealism of Viridiana with Jorge's hard-nosed materialism. When the newly arrived Jorge surveys the estate from a window its neglected fields stretching towards distant mountains seem a perfect image of Spain's own decay as a nation. Momentarily there is a sense of that peculiarly Spanish mixture of grandeur and wretchedness which, for instance, the poet Antonio Machado and the novelist Azorín often sought to capture. Indeed, the mood of the film, with its simultaneous abhorrence of and yet nostalgia for things traditionally Spanish, is very much indebted to the so-called 'Generation of 1898', the generation which preceded that of Buñuel and Lorca. As Jorge tells his mistress of his plans and of the hard work that lies ahead he is interrupted by the entrance of Viridiana below quixotically leading her band of beggars into the grounds. Even the beggars realise she is 'a little cranky', as one says under his breath (83), which would be an understatement no doubt of Jorge's first opinion of her. But it is a fine cinematic image which takes in from the balcony of the house all the desolation of the grounds, Viridiana and her beggars, and the sense of illusion in the remote mountains. This system of contrast continues when Jorge unexpectedly visits Viridiana in her room at night. Disturbed in the middle of prayer, Viridiana rushes the crown of thorns and other religious objects out of sight into a box, while Jorge, smoking, tells her he plans to have electricity installed (94). Contrasts between the nun and the mentality of the beggars are also sharply drawn. On one occasion the lame beggar, El Cojo, speaks piously to her about a picture of the Virgin he has painted, while almost in the same breath he makes a foul joke about La Cancionera, who had posed for the picture, being a most unsuitable model (96).

The most striking and cinematic juxtaposition, however, is the sequence dealing with the celebration of the Angelus in the fields. When the church bells toll six of the afternoon Viridiana claps her hands to summon the beggars to prayer (107). They kneel on the earth and murmur rhythmic response to Viridiana in the time-honoured pattern. In a very rapid montage the camera cuts continuously from the beggars at prayer to Jorge's feverishly industrious gang-workers who only a few dozen yards away are churning cement-mixers, tipping stones from a barrow, sawing timber and generally making the most strident noises. The successive juxtapositions thus operate on both a visual and auditory level. In the latter sense there is a very strong suggestion here of the past being shouted down as the prayerful murmurings are lost intermittently in the din of modern machinery. In the visual sense the contrast is between tranquillity - the static beggars under flowering almond trees - and the unambiguously violent movements of men and machines. In both senses the image is prophetic as regards Viridiana who will suffer violation and find it impossible to pursue religious calm. The sequence is so expressive it again recalls Lope's precept that a work should have a high point in its middle section which functions as an apex for the whole and to which all subsequent threads are tied. Certainly it is a fine example of the synthetic and paradigmatic image that Buñuel's insistent concentration upon objects is always likely to achieve. It may have been inspired by a remark Dalí made to Buñuel about Millet's famous painting of the Angelus, a painting Dalí despised and regarded as a symbol of impotence. But while impotence applies, there is also an unmistakable lyrical tenderness about Buñuel's Angelus and the treatment is not one-sided. This kind of ambivalence is typical in Buñuel and is especially noticeable in his treatment of character. His people are seldom wholly good or bad, but mixed and problematical, which is to say, human. Don Jaime is a case in point; his rescue of a drowning bee (50) is one of several illustrations of his better nature, while much the same applies to Jorge, for instance in his purchase of the leashed dog. As for Viridiana, there is no way of telling how much sensuality is latent in her brand of mysticism, and, as always in Buñuel, we have to make up our own minds.

The Angelus scene gives context to modern man's out-and-out materialism. Jorge is interested in electric as opposed to spiritual light, and, by the same token, it is the functional value of objects which appeals to him, as we see when he goes searching through junk in the attic for something useful (110). The beggars, on the other hand, are trapped between two worlds, having to pay lip-service to the divine in order to survive in the material world. The irony of their situation creates values which are distorted and contradictory. Capable of comradeship, even of tenderness, as in the example of Leproso stroking the white feathers of a dove with his warty hands (115), they are also intolerably proud, disrespectful of charity, jealous of their own pecking-order and inclined to the worst cruelty. Viridiana's offer of shelter only serves to exaggerate these contradictions for she takes away the one thing they did possess, freedom, which the beggar Pelón points out by quickly choosing to leave rather than accept her 'discipline' (85). It is only natural that when left alone in the house they revert to the most anarchic behaviour, anxious to make up for all their past privations in a materialist bacchanalia.

In this climactic sequence speed of montage reaches a new peak and the key note in Buñuel's treatment is spontaneity. Shots 144 to 175 depict the disintegration of order and values at the banquet table: the beggars eat, drink, dance and sing, but the wine spills, food is thrown, a child howls, two women fight, one is sexually assaulted and, finally, the blind man, in a fit of helpless rage and drunken jealousy, devastates the banquet table with his stick. Amid all this commotion occurs the now famous cinematic moment of the freeze, when, photographed by La Cancionera, the beggars appear in a still shot which is a replica of Da Vinci's 'Last Supper' (122). Without going into the multiple connotations of this paradigm, it will be clear that the freeze makes a literally stunning contrast with the beggars' otherwise frenzied movements, and this relates the essential vitality of their existence - futile and ephemeral as it may be - to a permanent and abstract dimension. Movement immediately returns and Leonardo's celebrated compositional values disintegrate in chaos as though confirming the principle of entropy. The previous part of the banquet scene had in fact been held together to some extent by the blind beggar's narrative, an account of how he shopped a crony to the police, which held everyone's attention. The telling of the story was, it is true, interrupted to great naturalistic effect by shots of wineglasses spilling, the phago-eroticism of greasy mouths devouring the sacrificial lamb, and by the subplot of the outcast Leper creeping in closer to get at the food. But the blind man's narrative at least gave some cohesion to the proceedings, thematic cohesion as well since betrayal is central to the Last Supper, to Viridiana's faith in the beggars being betrayed and to El Leproso's later murder of a comrade. After the Last Supper freeze there is nothing but the most calamitous movement as sexual instinct roused by drink runs riot. Enedina immediately lifts her skirts high to expose herself in front of the camera, and this, not the religious 'freeze', is the picture which La Cancionera in fact takes, another telling juxtaposition which amongst other things hints at misogynous elements in traditional morality. This provokes an assault upon her by Paco, during which the patriarchal Don Zequiel, whom Viridiana had unwisely left in charge, rises from his stupor to utter what is no doubt a perverse misquotation, possibly of St Augustine, 'Let them sin! So much better the repentance afterwards' (125), for which fine words he receives a faceful of custard in the more recent tradition of Laurel and Hardy. Meanwhile one further image stands out for its visual expressiveness, that of El Leproso clad in the bridal gown once so coveted by Don Jaime. This second dressing-up epitomises what is very literally the carnival spirit of the banquet, carnival being the last great blow-out before Lent and the bidding of farewell to the flesh, _carne vale_, an abstinence soon to be imposed on rather than chosen by the beggars. The Leper's ludicrous and repugnant interpretation of bridal innocence, dancing all the while to the blaring 'Messiah', indicates the extent to which values have been perverted. His bandaged hands hold the feathers of a dove, presumably the one he once cherished but has since killed, and as he throws the white feathers into the air like confetti there is an acute sense of the mindless violation done to innocence.

The long banquet sequence, together with the subsequent narrow squeak Viridiana and Jorge have with the crazed beggars, allows Buñuel to exploit film's natural facility for capturing frenetic movement, a facility the silent cinema quickly recognised. Though comic custard-pie elements are included, motion here has deeper implications. Primarily it conveys a sense of spontaneity, that is, uninhibited and free action, for the beggars are indeed free for a short while, as the contrast with Leonardo's forms forcefully shows. But the logical result of such freedom is chaos and devastation, captured in the frantic acceleration of pace. The destruction of the banquet table is an outward sign of this disintegration in values, it being ironic that in the materialist world objects seem to be valued less, or at least are valued only for their functional attributes, as with the crucifix which doubles as a flick-knife (125). When the evening's riotous events have run their course an abrupt change of pace is achieved by cutting from an exterior view of the house - its lit windows now complemented by the headlamps of a car - to a tranquil day scene in which a farm-hand leads two cows to pasture. But though this suggests permanence and continuity, there is no going back to the old values. In fact the objects and props which Buñuel introduces in the film's last minutes are singularly lacking in illusive or phantasmal connotations and instead point simply towards the emptiness of mundane reality: Viridiana sews like any woman;

she combs her hair looking into a glass whose cracked surface is a sign of her shattered dreams; finally the crown of thorns is burnt and she makes her way to Jorge's room where she sits to play cards with him and Ramona. This last sequence, though not Buñuel's original choice, is a far more effective way of ending the film than the erotic scene to which the censor took exception. It hints at a ménage à trois but at the same time brings an air of disillusionment and devitalisation appropriate to Viridiana's mood. It might be compared with the ending to Lorca's poem 'The Gypsy Nun', where, for different reasons, a nun has her dreams crushed and now listlessly watches 'the light playing at chess on the lattice window'. [14] Like chess, the card game suggests an attempt to escape life's tedium and oppression, but the game itself is likely to be just as repetitious and empty and it will certainly oblige those who play to adhere to its rules and regulations.

At the film's end Viridiana is poised for a new start in life, much like the later pugnacious female, Tristana. But the future which awaits is forbidding, more so for Viridiana who has been stripped of all idealism. She has learnt that she cannot escape the real world where freedom, especially a woman's freedom, is restricted if not entirely illusory. This she accepts, her decision to visit Jorge being a surrender in more senses than one. Most important, however, is that the film's whole technique has prepared us for such a resigned ending. The depiction of objects, upon which the film's articulation is firmly based, is the key to this fatalism. On the one hand, certain selected objects have been the emblem of dreams, both for Viridiana and the pathetic Don Jaime, while the transformational nature of the medium has helped give texture to their aspirations. But on the other hand, the incessant repetition of objects - such as the skipping-rope, the tree, the crown of thorns, the fire motif, the various animals, the gramophone and its music, the bridal outfit - has created a totally integrated and therefore, ultimately, closed pattern. Insistent repetition, supported in the broader aspects of montage by the day-night cycles, by the twofold transvestism and the twofold abuse of Viridiana, results in what is possibly Buñuel's most finely conceived and most rhythmic film. But it is a rhythm so tightly interlocked that it ultimately expresses the fundamental pessimism which he says Surrealism taught him, namely, that 'man is not free'.[15] In short, it appears that our dreams are no more than phantoms and we are obliged to live in the cold world of objects.

ROBERT G. HAVARD

University College of Wales
Aberystwyth

NOTES

1 The controversy which the cinema provoked in Spain is outlined in C.B. Morris, This Loving Darkness (Hull/Oxford, 1980). Buñuel's references to the 'seventh art' are found in Francisco de Aranda, Luis Buñuel: Biografía crítica (Barcelona, 1969), 314, 328.

2 '... nuestras injustísimas instituciones sociales, como la religión, la patria, la familia, la cultura, en fin, los llamados "pilares" de la sociedad', Luis Buñuel, Viridiana, 4th edition (Mexico, 1976), 6.

3 'Quisiera ser un cisne. Pero no puedo aunque quisiera. Porque, ¿dónde dejaría mi sombrero? ¿Dónde mi cuello de pajarita y mi corbata de moaré? ¡Qué desgracia!', El paseo de Buster Keaton, F. García Lorca, Obras completas, 19th edition (Madrid 1974), 235-6.

4 '¡Qué esfuerzo!
¡Qué esfuerzo del caballo por ser perro!
¡Qué esfuerzo del perro por ser golondrina!
¡Qué esfuerzo de la golondrina por ser abeja!
¡Qué esfuerzo de la abeja por ser caballo!
... Y yo, por los aleros,
¡qué serafín de llamas busco y soy!'

F. García Lorca, Obras completas, 503.

5 'trampas, celdas, cavernas encantadas,
pajareras y cuartos numerados,
todos se transfiguran, todos vuelan,
cada moldura es nube, cada puerta
da al mar, al campo, al aire, cada mesa
es un festín ...
todo se transfigura y es sagrado ...'

Octavio Paz, 'Piedra de sol', Libertad bajo palabra, (Mexico, 1968), 247.

6 '... me hace saltar'. Here and elsewhere the number in parentheses indicates the page of reference in Luis Buñuel, Viridiana, 4th edition (Mexico, 1976).

7 Luis Buñuel, Tristana, English translation by Nicholas Fry (New York, 1971), 55-6.

8 'La mujer honrada, pierna quebrada, y en casa', ibid., 48.

9 'Arrojóme las naranjicas,
con los ramos del blanco azahar;
arrojómelas y arrojéselas,
y volviómelas a arrojar.'

See D. Alonso and J.M. Blecus, Antología de la poesía española, Lírica de tipo tradicional (Madrid, 1969), 94.

10 'Monjica en religión
me quiero entrar,
por no malmaridar.'

11 See Luis Buñuel, Mi último suspiro (Barcelona, 1982), 97, 227.

12 Ibid., 212.

13 Roland Barthes, Sade/Fourier/Loyala (London, 1977).

14 'La luz juega el ajedrez
alto de la celosía.'

F.G. Lorca, 'La monja gitana', Obras completas, 405.

15 See The World of Luis Buñuel, edited by Joan Mellen (New York, 1978), 252.

MYTH AND RITUAL IN <u>BELLE DE JOUR</u>

Though less complicated in structure than, for example, *The Phantom of Liberty* or *The Discreet Charm of the Bourgeoisie*, *Belle de Jour* displays Buñuel's distinctive interest in structural experiment. Here the contrasting worlds of reason and desire are explored not only through the clash between consciousness and dream (or daydream), but also through the comparisons between life at the brothel and the social reality beyond.

Like the fort in Ford's westerns, Séverine's flat in the 'normal' outside world is offered to us as a place of ambivalent status: it is at once an image of order, security, warmth (the tidiness of the flat, its depiction as a place of refuge from menacing characters like Husson, the glowing fire in the hearth), and also a setting for repression and trauma (the memory of being sexually molested by the workman takes place in the bathroom, Séverine knocks over the roses in the sitting room, sexual distance is usually imposed in the bedroom). The values that are dominant in this bourgeois flat, in this bourgeois marriage between a doctor (a healer of bodies but not of minds) and an elegant lady with time on her hands, spread over into the social life they lead, but as with the image of their married life, so too in the picture of bourgeois holidays, pastimes, social gatherings we are made to see the underside of the image of perfection and purity so carefully created by dominant ideology and so neatly reproduced in the film by Buñuel.

In the landau at the very beginning of the film, as Séverine is being propelled towards humiliation and cruelty, Pierre earnestly remarks that he wishes everything could be perfect in their lives. 'Parfait' is a word he chooses with some care; it evokes memories not only of Neoplatonic types of love (devoid, at the highest level, of physical consummation), but also of more determinedly spiritual recommendations concerning self-improvement. Quite evidently Buñuel expects us to see in Pierre's search for perfection an element of the ridiculous, since even St Teresa of Avila knew, if the Way of Perfection is anything to go by, that perfection exists in heaven alone.

For Buñuel an ideal of perfection is typically bourgeois in its sneering and in any case only superficial distaste for materialism. Perfection does not exist: the Ambassador of the Republic of Miranda, in The Discreet Charm of the Bourgeoisie, on the surface devoted only to the 'higher' things of life is, when he is not dreaming about filling his belly, trying to seduce the wife of one of his best friends.

And so too in Belle de Jour surface purity, or 'perfection', is juxtaposed with inward baseness or turmoil. The unmistakable pattern of white clothes and objects draws our attention to the dual perspective of Buñuel's interest in the safety of the outside world, the apparently ordered, spotless and secure world of a bourgeoise: on the one hand white is used for Pierre's pyjamas, his polo-neck sweater at the skiing resort, his medical overalls at the hospital, Séverine's underwear, her tennis clothes, her gown in two of the dreams, and is of course the dominant colour of the skiing resort setting, but on the other hand, white is also the colour of heroin, the 'neige' that Hippolyte and Marcel are expecting to pick up from the gangsters, and, significantly, when Husson turns up at the brothel, among the things he remembers from his last visit is not only that the central heating was 'au maximum' but also that it was snowing. Not only then an indication of purity, white is also a reminder that this is a sterile (the medical allusions in the film emphasise this), not to say profoundly hypocritical and evil world. It is fascinating to notice, moreover, that as Buñuel swamps us with these images of purity, he simultaneously begins to create another pattern of colours deliberately designed to elucidate and strengthen the irony of the pattern of whites. Our first view of Séverine sees her dressed in scarlet; a typical joke, as Séverine dreams of herself as the inveterate 'scarlet woman' of literature and history. Scarlet is only worn again by her quite late on in the film, this time at a point where she has become a leading figure operating at ease and with power and skill at the brothel. How different from her first appearance there when dressed in sombre dark grey she not only through choice of colour betrays a desire for anonymity before violating one of her society's major taboos, but also demonstrates the extent to which in wearing clothes whose colour exactly matches his she is the plaything of M. Husson.

Séverine is, of course, not the only dreamer in the film - the maid at the brothel informs Husson, 'je rêve de vous' - nor are her dreams Buñuel's major focus of interest. Even though we do not see him dreaming, or daydreaming, like the maid or like Séverine, Husson is the film's most important dreamer, if we take the dream as metaphor and expand it within a figurative context. Indeed, without Husson's 'dreams' of havoc none of the others would dream in the way they do.

Formally Husson is a reincarnation of the Devil from the autos sacramentales, or his secular equivalent, Calderón's Basilio in La vida es sueño. Before Husson's words ring in Séverine's ear, informing her of Mme Anaïs' address, Buñuel makes his holidaymakers at the skiing resort (Pierre, Séverine, Renée) engage in conversation about hypnotists. The point of the conversation only becomes apparent when Husson's words about the brothel are heard ringing in Séverine's ears, as if hypnotising her and compelling her to make her way to his accomplice in havoc, Mme Anaïs. Once hypnotised, victims act as if in a dream. In this sense is Husson a dreamer: a maker of dreams, where individuals are deprived of their freedom even when they most urgently believe they are discovering it.

Husson's dream is the nightmare of bourgeois life; he is an embodiment of idleness, wealth, sexual depravity, and is therefore, as Buñuel wittily puts it, suffering from some physical (though we would want to say ideological) ailment. He is the representation of the underside of bourgeois morality and religion and whereas to a man, enjoying some of the benefits of these, he is only 'drôle' and therefore harmless (as Pierre describes him early on in the film), to a woman suffering to a greater or lesser extent as a consequence of the imposition of institutions dedicated to sexual discrimination, he is either 'bizarre', as Séverine from a position of relative distance puts it, or 'pire que ça', as from a position of nearness and therefore knowledge, Renée is able to verify. She is, after all, the woman with scars on her wrists.

If Husson's words ring in a woman's ears, or, in other words, if women are in the grip of bourgeois ideals, hypnotised and turned into dreamers stripped of freedom of choice and will, what becomes of them? The first answer Buñuel gives is that they become traumatised and frigid. As he formulates his answer in the film one can see Freud standing over his shoulder.

Like Hitchcock's Marnie, Buñuel's Séverine is 'severe' with men, frigid, in some respects child-like, and immobilised by the traumatic experiences of her childhood. Unlike Marnie whose experiences led her to loathe men, Séverine finds herself attracted to them in a way she has been taught to regard as degenerate. If sex is equated with dirt, a bourgeoise cannot possibly be expected to favour it. (It is surely not without significance that her first sexual encounter is with a workman wearing soiled overalls). Afraid of Pierre's opinion of her, once he became familiar with her desire, she keeps her longings to herself, not knowing that Pierre himself may be as equally confused sexually in his relationships towards her, as she clearly is towards him. It may be, for instance, that in marrying Séverine Pierre has not only been attracted to a bourgeois ideal of beauty and elegance but has also succumbed to a woman whose image has been carefully created to arouse conflicting sadistic and protective impulses in a man. Like Mark Rutland in Marnie he rises to the challenge of frigidity, so that he may conquer where none had found success before; also like Rutland he may well enjoy the part of father that this child-like wife seems eager for him to play. Séverine refuses to go to sleep early on in the film unless Pierre agrees to sit beside her until she drops off. There is too some irony in Husson's remarks about Séverine's appearance at the very end of the film: as he arrives to reveal all to Pierre, Husson tells Séverine that she looks like a 'collégienne précoce'. Just so; some of her sexual problems may have been solved, but socially she is still a child, still restricted to the playing of childish roles in society and still, therefore, as her clothes also resemble those of the maid, a subservient creature in a patriarchally-constructed world. Perhaps it is, after all, the child-like qualities in Séverine that have drawn Pierre to her, cancelling as they do lingering fears of castration. Here is another blonde whose potential menace and power have been contained, not through humour, but through fetishization and the imposition of an image of childishness on her social reality.

In discussing film and literary blondes, Leslie Fiedler, Angela Carter and Richard Dyer have in their own fashion usefully drawn attention to the ways in which culture extols the beauty of attractive women through techniques that also demolish their threat and power.[1] It is as though the knight's recognition - in the fairy story about the loathly damsel - that power over men is what women do most desire becomes an idea that haunts all men who celebrate the beauty of women. Jayne Mansfield's threat is contained through parody, Mae West's through age, Marilyn Monroe's through childishness, that of Hitchcock's heroines through fetishization, and Séverine's through a mixture of some of these attitudes. Like Silvia Pinal, Delphine Seyrig, Simone Signoret, Catherine Deneuve is a Buñuel blonde taunting men into slavery, but trapped herself by an ideology from which there appears no escape. The blonde-child has a momentary reign of power, like Lolita and Baby Doll, and she can be tyrannical, naughty or wilful for a while, but the setting for her sovereignty is only a fashion house (the sign outside Mme Anaïs' flat is 'modes'), where everyone is merely acting out a part (the gynaecologist rebukes his whore for missing out part of the dialogue), and roles last only as long as the costume is in place, which in Séverine's case is certainly not beyond five o'clock. ('De deux heures à cinq heures, mais pas plus tard que cinq heures').

Séverine's time at the brothel is in fact thought by her to be a necessary stage in her proper education for life in the world of 'normality', and for marriage to Pierre. The film seems to invoke Freud's remarks in the essay on the taboo of virginity concerning the real motives for Judith's decapitation of Holofernes. [2] Freud talks first about the trauma, anxieties, fears caused by the loss of virginity in primitive communities, and draws attention to the way in which a bride's defloration is frequently ritualized and left in the hands of a group of women, a holy person, or some such 'official' so that the possibly malign consequences of the act shall not fall on the head of the husband. Judith, he argues, conceals precisely such a sexual motive - of ridding a husband of the implications of defloration - beneath a political act, the slaying of a man who threatens her people. As Holofernes is decapitated by Judith, decapitation becomes a symbol of castration. Buñuel himself uses decapitation as castration in <u>Tristana</u> when in her dream Tristana sees the head of her guardian and seducer hanging instead of the clapper in a huge church bell. If Séverine is a child - though perhaps only figuratively - then possibly - also perhaps only figuratively - she is still a virgin. It is on the heads of her clients at the brothel that she will bring down the malign consequences of her defloration and not on that of her husband Pierre, whom, she confirms to Marcel, she loves, and beside whom she expects to take up her place as a respectable wife.

The complicated and contradictory motives that draw Séverine momentarily away from Pierre are aptly exposed at the brothel. It is, of course, at a fairly low level, a place of elucidation. Séverine is christened 'Belle de jour' by Mme Anaïs, and so that we do not miss the 'jour' in concentrating too hard on the 'belle', Buñuel makes everyone say 'bon jour' - in all, three times - when Séverine makes her first professional appearance. 'Qui êtes-vous?' Séverine is asked by one of the other girls later on, and although she never replies we know that she has at the brothel finally begun to ask herself the same question as well. At another level, the brothel is a heightened expression of the normal world outside. If the gangster world of classical Hollywood movies made in that genre is actually a baroque expression of an only slightly distorted image of the world of capitalism and 'business' in ordinary life, the call-girl milieu of Belle de Jour clarifies the nature of certain aspects of many sexual relationships in the world outside. The underside of 'normality' is here brought to the surface. There are many ways in which Buñuel makes deliberate formal links between the outer and inner worlds of brothel and normality; 'Belle de Jour' in the inner world is matched by 'Belle de l'ombre' in the outer one (cat symbolism helping to draw attention to traditional and enervating associations between women and cats and evil sexuality, such as are also invoked in films like Cat People, The Spirit of the Beehive and so on); the child motif, concerning Séverine in the outside world, is picked up in the depiction of Marcel in the inner one (Hippolyte calls him 'mon petit', refers to him as a son, Marcel himself says that tracking down Séverine back to her flat is 'enfantin', and the clue in the cross-word puzzle one of the girls is doing at the brothel is concerned with Aeneas and Anchises); sunglasses are worn in the outside world by Séverine, the Duke's butler, and by Pierre at the end of the film, and by Husson when he visits the brothel.

Normality and abnormality are therefore indistinguishable; the brothel exposes what in many instances is the legalised prostitution of the world outside. The only difference at the brothel is, as Angela Carter puts it, that the woman 'makes a realistic assessment of her assets, and does not have to rely on fraud to make a living'.[3] While all the other women engaged in prostitution in the film do so purely for the money, and therefore in order to achieve economic independence, Séverine, though also doing it for the money, as she explains to the Duke, is also prostituting herself for other reasons, including the desire for rebirth after a preliminary but essential process of self-destruction.

Like Mallarmé's swan in the poem, 'Le vierge, le vivace, et le bel aujourd'hui', made, by culture, pure, white, virginal, Séverine is isolated (like Nazarín and Robinson Crusoe), and as if trapped in a lake of ice at the dawning of a '<u>bel</u> au<u>jour</u>d'hui'. To free herself (and most of Buñuel's characters are searching for freedom of various types), she must descend into an underworld, the hidden, secret, womb-like world of the brothel. The brothel is, too, a kind of sea of chaos, where Séverine is a pearl - as Anaïs and Hippolyte both agree - growing again in the dark, receptive finally to forces and instincts that are considered degenerate on the surface of bourgeois life. If we compare this figurative sea with the literal image of the sea we are given when Séverine and Pierre are on holiday on the second occasion in the film we cannot help but notice that while in the latter - a reminder of much Surrealist art, such as Tanguy's for instance - the sea is forbidding, and its aura of hostility, matched by a leafless, dead tree-trunk, represents the dessicated life of Séverine's marriage to Pierre, the former, if we can judge by her growing confidence in dealing with her clients, seems, on the surface at least, to be a more productive and fertile kind of experience. Here Séverine does indeed become a kind of pearl: no longer virginal (pearls, it should be recalled, are attributes of the Virgin Mary), but valuable, and prepared to go down any road for the sake of knowledge (for Spanish audiences the references to pearls in Don Gil de las calzas verdes would surely summon up associations of androgyny, homosexuality and role reversals, and make them applicable to Belle de Jour).

Like Judith, though, Belle de Jour prepares to resume her life in the outside world. Séverine eventually triumphs over Belle, and Buñuel's play with time prepares us for that eventuality.

Buñuel's use of time in Belle de Jour serves both as a means of disorientating the viewer (as it does at the very outset of his career in Un Chien Andalou, where time structures complement other types of assault on the preconceptions of the viewer), and as a way of drawing our attention to the interdependence of the film's fictive inner and outer worlds. An underlying assumption in most of Buñuel's films is that redemption is possible through the destruction of the artificial order of chronos, or clock-time, which is frequently used as an image of habit. This is a secularised version of the mystic's escape from time, when at the highest stage of his or her inner journey towards God apprehension of truth, of reality, is accessible through what are defined as supra-rational means. In an instant the mystic is displaced from clock-time and sees eternity, where things exist in essence, rather than in sequence.

In Belle de Jour the brothel provides just such an opportunity for liberation from time, or, in other words, the social habits and order of the world outside, personified by M. Husson, whose first remark in the film is a question about the time: 'Quelle heure est-il?' (The reply is, significantly, given Séverine's work from two to five at the brothel, five o'clock.) The brothel is, in Mircea Eliade's terminology, a 'sacred place', a topsy-turvy image of primitive man's place apart, for the celebration and ritualization of mysteries, communication with gods, the consideration of higher things, all outside the constraints of time and place in the ordinary world.[4]

Yet Séverine is always conscious of clock-time, always has one eye on the hour of her departure and her return to bourgeois life. The brothel does not make her rebel against that life, does not make her see the triviality of the life she leads in her smart flat, taking holidays with empty-headed friends, and it fails to make her recognise the narcissistic, self-satisfied nature of her bourgeois marriage. The awareness she gains at the brothel is, after all, only limited. The brothel is not Utopia; it could hardly be that, since Buñuel shows us that it is not only a place of illusions but also ultimately a place ruled by the spirit of M. Husson.[5]

The girls at the brothel, even Mme Anaïs, only have power in the way that the women at Sade's castle of pleasures and vices have power: for a limited period, like actors and actresses momentarily playing at being authoritarian duchesses trampling on inefficient lackeys. As in Genet's The Balcony, where a bishop turns out to be a gas-man, so here a lackey turns out to be a gynaecologist and we are never in any doubt that the clients are in command.[6] The male clients say who wears what in this place of fashion, and although Séverine discovers here that sexual pleasure has deep-grown social implications, and begins uninhibitedly to discover her own sexuality, Buñuel shows us through her portrayal that the ideologically contaminated find cures with difficulty. Among the things that Séverine never discovers is that her 'taste for pain' comes from Husson, that her own deviant condition can only be made intelligible within the context of social patterns.[7]

Husson, Buñuel's embodiment of dominant ideology's darker side, is, fittingly, Séverine's last client. The paradise of death that he creates - through the planting of Asphodels - is eternally in bloom, there to trap more and more Séverines: not only Henriette, but also the maid's daughter at the brothel, whose attraction for the Korean recalls the young Séverine's for the workman.[8] Like the Marquis de Sade, M. Husson gives women temporary power, celebrates in women a sexuality detached from reproductive functions, creates an atmosphere where women are able to overcome feelings of shame and disgust, but the final goal of such freedom is of course further enslavement. We know that Séverine remains prey to dominant beliefs about gender and role because the dream that Husson plants in her mind is a self-destructive dream of physical, but also by extension moral, masochism. Husson's third remark in the film is an expression of pleasure at the sight of the scars on Renée's wrists. Cruelty to women is what Husson relishes, and that is subsequently what Séverine is forced to admit she likes too. In other words, just as his voice rings in her ear with the address of Mme Anaïs' brothel, so too is a taste for pain inflicted on Séverine by the sadist Husson. Séverine's dream is Buñuel's expression of a tyrannical society's addiction to subjugation, displacement and cruelty. If we accept that Husson, as the personification of the contradictions of social conditions, controls the dreams of all - like the Marquis de Sade, like Basilio and the Devil in Calderón's plays, like the _meneur de jeu_ in Ophuls' _La Ronde_ - Sêverine is quite clearly a manufactured masochist, created by social conditions to hanker after self-destruction.[9] If we deny Husson status of this kind, as the originator of Sêverine's, and, by extension, all women's masochism, we would be obliged to construct an image of Buñuel himself as a man imposing his own sadistic fantasies on his dumb blonde, and, given the evidence of his career as an iconoclast of the bourgeoisie, we would hardly want to do that.[10]

PETER W. EVANS

University of Newcastle
upon Tyne

NOTES

1 See Leslie A. Fiedler, Love and Death in the American Novel (London, 1967), Angela Carter, The Sadeian Woman (London, 1979), and Richard Dyer, Marilyn Monroe, B.F.I. Star Dossier 1 (London, 1980).

2 See Sigmund Freud, On Sexuality, translated by James Strachey and edited by Angela Richards (Harmondsworth, 1977), pp. 261-83.

3 See op. cit., p. 58.

4 See Mircea Eliade, Patterns in Comparative Religion (London, 1958).

5 In 'Buñuel's Golden Bowl', included in Robert Adkinson's translation of the script of Belle de Jour (London, 1971), p. 20, Elliot Stein takes a different view, and argues that by the end of the film Séverine is no longer a bourgeoise.

6 Comparisons between Buñuel and Genet are made by Andrew Sarris in Adkinson's edition of the film script, op. cit., pp. 21-28.

7 I take the phrase from the title of Maria Marcus' interesting but ultimately unsatisfactory book, A Taste for Pain. On Masochism and Female Sexuality (London, 1978). A penetrating, but necessarily short discussion of the subject is Ros Coward's 'Erin Pizzey Adrift in a Misogynist Society', The Guardian, 2nd November 1982.

8 A remark made by Pam Cook about Mildred Pierce, in 'Duplicity in Mildred Pierce', from Women in Film Noir, edited by E. Ann Kaplan (London, 1978), p. 81, 'we have another image of sacrifice which closes the film with a reminder of what women must give up for the sake of the patriarchal order', seems appropriate in the context of the Korean's attentions on the maid's daughter in Belle de Jour.

9 See Pam Cook, op. cit., on the way women's voices are silenced in film noir, and Deborah Thomas on the role of the meneur de jeu in La Ronde, in Movie, 29-30 (Summer, 1982), pp. 73-79.

10 I am indebted for awards from the British Academy and the University of Newcastle upon Tyne which made it possible for me to visit Buñuel in Mexico and undertake this research.